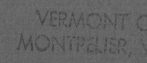

NEW FRONTIERS OF THE AMERICAN RECONSTRUCTION

NEW FRONTIERS
OF THE AMERICAN
RECONSTRUCTION

Edited by Harold M. Hyman

WITHDRAWN

UNIVERSITY OF ILLINOIS PRESS, URBANA • CHICAGO • LONDON, 1966

PREFACE
AND ACKNOWLEDGMENTS
1965 RECONSTRUCTION
CONFERENCE PROCEEDINGS

"No one has so far called for a commemoration of Reconstruction," Professor C. Vann Woodward noted in December, 1965.[1] Probably no one will, at least in the forms in which since 1961 the major military events of the Civil War have received centennial observation. Odds are that few Americans today believe that the men and measures of the Reconstruction deserve celebration in a commendatory manner.

It was not always so. Many contemporaries of Abraham Lincoln and of Andrew Johnson looked on a reconstruction of the Union as an opportunity for improving certain conditions of American life. As example, the educator Daniel Coit Gilman in 1867 wrote that "the present epoch of 're-construction'" meant opportunity for "young men bent on progress."[2]

---

[1] New York *Times Book Review*, December 5, 1965, p. 54.

[2] Daniel Coit Gilman to Charles Eliot Norton, November 2, 1867, quoted in Hugh Hawkins, *Pioneer, a History of the Johns Hopkins University, 1874–1889* (Ithaca, N.Y., 1960), p. 18.

But by the turn of the century popular and scholarly judgments had shifted so much to an opposite point of view that in 1901, in an in-group jest to Frederic Bancroft, the historian William A. Dunning wrote: "Lord, how the reconstructors have been reconstructed! I'm going to . . . take the ground that the whole [Reconstruction] business was ethically, socially, and politically right; that's the only way in which a man can attract any attention now."[3]

However, in published writings Dunning and his numerous, talented, and durable students helped to build the twentieth century's consensus that almost everything connected with the Reconstruction was a tragic error.[4]

Although this derogatory view holds on with remarkable tenacity, historians, including many from the South, for decades have been chipping away at it. Especially in recent years the pace has quickened of fruitful reevaluations of the dim and gory terrain of the historiography of the Reconstruction period.[5] A result is that a form of commemoration of the Reconstruction has come into being. Its spirit is that of the seminar more than of the pageant. Improved understanding through continuing scholarship is its goal.

---

[3] William A. Dunning to Frederic Bancroft, April 5, 1901, Frederic Bancroft Papers, Special Collections, Columbia University Library.

[4] In the introduction to my *The Radical Republicans and Reconstruction, 1861–1870* (Indianapolis, 1966), I have attempted to survey the causes and development of these attitudes.

[5] So swift is this pace that while this book was in press, new scholarship appeared in print that I am sure one or more contributors to the conference of which the present volume is the proceedings would have welcomed opportunity to use, but could not. These latecomer items include: David Donald, *The Politics of Reconstruction, 1863–1867* (Baton Rouge, 1965); George M. Frederickson, *The Inner Civil War: Northern Intellectuals and the Crisis of the Union* (New York, 1965); William Gillette, *The Right to Vote: Politics and the Passage of the Fifteenth Amendment* (Baltimore, 1965); Philip Van Doren Stern, *When the Guns Roared: World Aspects of the American Civil War* (Garden City, N.Y., 1965).

In this spirit and with aim at this goal, a Reconstruction Conference convened in April, 1965, at the University of Illinois. Men who are involved in research that centers on the Reconstruction theme came from locations scattered across this country and from Canada. These historians offered papers on their discrete subjects, and commentaries and criticisms on the papers were presented by other participants. All who were involved in planning this conference hoped that the audience would make itself an integral part of the proceedings. To that end, invitations to attend the sessions of the conference went out to many individuals and to departments of history in secondary schools, colleges, and universities, as well as to the faculty and student body of the University of Illinois, and with happy result. In some instances people came from very far away. Members of the large audience participated freely and usefully in the discussions that followed the presentations of the papers and of the commentaries on the papers. Perhaps this interaction helped better to define some of the new frontiers of Reconstruction research and to mark areas of improved information and interpretation we think we have won.

Someone had to pay for the advantages derived from this ingathering. President David Dodds Henry and Vice-President Lyle Lanier of the University of Illinois provided the funds for the conference. They also encouraged the enterprise so enthusiastically as to make almost pleasurable my double burden of organizing it and of participating in a session. I am grateful to them, and to other University administrative officials who coped so well with the care and feeding of historians. My colleagues Professors Geoffrey Bruun (visiting), Norman Graebner, Robert Johannsen, and Winton Solberg helped to resolve many questions that came up in organizing the venture, and graced the ceremonies as chairmen of the several sessions. Professor Robert Waller permitted me to exploit his ongoing work in liaison with secondary school teachers of history in Illinois, with result that news of the conference reached many persons who usually fail to hear of such events at the University and who attend them even more rarely. I am grateful also to the University of Illinois Library for presenting an exhibit of printed materials on Reconstruction simultaneously with this conference, and to the staff of the University Press for their fine work in the preparation of the announcements for the conference and now of this volume. My wife, Ferne B. Hyman, helped to make perfect the conference arrangements for the visiting participants, and I give her special thanks.

Harold M. Hyman
Baltimore
February, 1966

CONTENTS

RECONSTRUCTION AND POLITICAL-CONSTITUTIONAL INSTITUTIONS: THE POPULAR EXPRESSION
HAROLD M. HYMAN 1

Comment on Harold M. Hyman's Paper
ALFRED H. KELLY 40

RECONSTRUCTION AND THE NEGRO
JOHN HOPE FRANKLIN 59

Comment on John Hope Franklin's Paper
AUGUST MEIER 77

SOUTH AMERICA LOOKS AT NORTH AMERICAN RECONSTRUCTION
HARRY BERNSTEIN 87

CANADA AND RECONSTRUCTION, 1863–79
W. L. MORTON 105

SEEDS OF FAILURE IN RADICAL RACE POLICY

C. VANN WOODWARD 125

Comment on C. Vann Woodward's Paper

RUSSEL B. NYE 148

RECONSTRUCTION AND POLITICAL-CONSTITUTIONAL INSTITUTIONS: THE POPULAR EXPRESSION

HAROLD M. HYMAN
University of Illinois

"We must live in the world the [Civil] War made," Sidney Breese, the Chief Justice of Illinois, wrote early in 1877 to a trusted political henchman in Springfield.[1]

What *were* the war-altered configurations of the American constitutional-political world to which Breese adverted? Some thoughtful men, looking backward from the 1870's and 1880's, especially as centennial observations of American independence and constitution-framing appeared, understood that the stirring events of the 1860's had been watershed and crossroads, leading to alterations.

Ably expressing this concept, the canny publicist E. L.

---

[1] Sidney Breese to Reuben Benjamin, January 3, 1877, owned by and used with permission of Mr. W. R. Benjamin, Chicago. All workers in the arena of Civil War constitutional history base their efforts on the foundations set in James G. Randall's *Constitutional Problems Under Lincoln*, published first in 1926 and issued in a revised edition in 1951 by the University of Illinois Press. Instead of referring continually in this paper to Professor Randall's precedent work, I state here my debt to it.

Godkin in 1887 examined the failure of American institutions in 1860–61, culminating in secession and war. The Constitution had been partially "provisional," "experimental," and defective as it came out of Philadelphia a century earlier, Godkin believed. Its defects had made possible the strains set up by the champions of slavery's extension and perpetualization and by worshipers at the shrine of primary state allegiance.

Godkin asserted that before 1861 political, not constitutional, institutions tried to cope with the great questions which had unsettled American politics since the 1790's — the Alien and Sedition acts, the embargo, the tariff, internal improvements, the national banking system, as well as slavery extension. Then secession in 1860–61 swept all other public matters into the background. By 1865 the war, reshaping the nation's institutional relationships, created a slaveless nation out of the congeries of uncertainties that staggered to secession in 1861.

State sovereignty — the "lower law" of the Constitution in the telling phrase of the Boston *Commonwealth* — was the happy casualty of Appomattox. Thereafter the world knew that a nation held sway in the United States. Godkin asserted in 1887 that the heroes of 1865 completed the task left unfinished by the too-timid framers of 1787 and concluded with the suggestion "that those who celebrate the next centennial of the Constitution will be disposed to put the date in 1865, rather than in 1787, or will at all events hesitate between the two years." As further bonus, after Appomattox the congressional framers of the Reconstruction amendments "took hold resolutely of all the seriously obscure or ambiguous passages in the instrument, and of all compromises which had proved difficult or incapable of execution, and eliminated them."[2]

---

[2] E. L. Godkin, "Some Things Overlooked at the Centennial," *The Nation* (September 22, 1887), p. 226.

With another centennial at hand, Godkin's epigrammatic suggestion is particularly attractive; dating the Constitution's birth or at least maturity from 1865 instead of 1787 is a reasonable way of looking at the past. Appomattox did settle basic questions which had kept American politics upset for forty years before 1860 and which finally ripped the nation apart at Sumter, presumably forever. What follows is an attempt to reconsider, as a constructive episode in American constitutional life, the period secession through Reconstruction.

My predecessor at the University of Illinois in the study of American constitutional history, Professor Arthur Bestor, who now graces the History faculty at the University of Washington, has written that the direction the war took "was determined by the pre-existing form of the constitutional system. . . . It was constitutional theorizing, carried on from the very birth of the Republic, which made secession the ultimate recourse of any group that considered its vital interests threatened." As with Godkin's, I carry Bestor's concept a step along to suggest that the constitutional concepts underlying Reconstruction took firm form very soon after Sumter, not after Appomattox.[3]

Professor Bestor's lucid and useful overview offers an analytical scheme so logical as to inspire wonder in the blindness of men a century ago not to know where they were, why and how they had gotten there, and what paths into the future they should take. The fact, of course, is that even informed men in 1860 were astonished at being suddenly involved in crisis, however long tensions had been building toward headlines. Adverting in 1887 to this sense of unpreparedness, United States Senator William B. Allison, whose uninter-

---

[3] Arthur Bestor, "The American Civil War as a Constitutional Crisis," *American Historical Review*, LXIX (January, 1964), 329.

rupted congressional service stretched back to 1862, told the graduating class of the State University of Iowa:

When some future Tacitus shall record our annals, it will be difficult for him to explain to the student of our government how it was possible for . . . [slavery] to attain such proportions under a free constitution, and such mastery over a free people; and especially will he wonder by what process of alluring sophistry this high court [the Supreme Court of the United States] could have its eyes so dazed, and its intellect so blurred, as to seek [in the Dred Scott case] to enthrone in the constitution the spirit of slavery, where the spirit of liberty had dwelt before.[4]

If men close to the heart of public affairs were shocked by the virulent form the slavery issue assumed as the 1860's opened, although it had been the center of contention for forty years, how much more startling to the general American public the *act* of secession seemed. As a repeated threat from the South, the idea of secession had become blunted from overuse. But as a reality it was a stunningly unexpected foul blow.[5]

Proceeding unopposed, secession was not merely a political

---

[4] William B. Allison, *The Strength of Our Government: An Address at the Commencement of the State University of Iowa, June 22, 1887* (Iowa City, 1887), p. 11.

[5] The Illinois theologian J. M. Sturtevant, "The Lessons of Our National Conflict," *New Englander*, XIX (October, 1861), 894–912, wrote: "It is, perhaps, the most remarkable characteristic of our present national adversity that it has overtaken us unawares. The public mind did not anticipate it and was not prepared for it. We were enjoying unexampled national prosperity and we were taking it for granted that we should enjoy it forever. Wars, commotions, and revolutions we thought were for less favored lands, but for us an uninterrupted future of peaceful growth. These were but the delusive dreams of our national childhood. . . . We are now called to learn the lessons of adversity" (p. 894). Secession and war were teaching "admiration and respect for a strong and energetic government" (p. 896). See also Paul C. Nagel, *One Nation Indivisible: The Union in American Thought; 1776–1861* (New York, 1964), pp. 287–88.

crisis in the operation of the Constitution but the termination of constitutional and political operations. The incapacity of national institutions to stem the centrifugal tide appeared to validate the South's charges that so little vigor obtained in the Union as to make too dear whatever cost adhered to continuing membership.

Today it is difficult to recapture the mood of pessimism concerning the capacity of American institutions to survive secession that blanketed the unbellicose North as 1860 gave way to 1861. Resistance as at Fort Sumter was hardly likely and occurred there out of accident; an Appomattox capitulation was wildly out of the context of possibility. Secession was the dreadfully public admission of the nation's failure to solve the slavery question through rational means, as every other slaveowning society, including the despised Latin American countries, had already done or was in process of accomplishing.

Worse, unopposed secession was the confirmation of a century of conservative doomsaying here and abroad on the incapacity of federalism and of democracy to work and on the undesirability of their existence. The turbulent, optimistic age of Jackson was closing with a whimper. Bets were high against an age of Lincoln succeeding it, especially with the aged Buchanan serving as interim placeholder.

How could odds go other ways? As 1860 gave way to 1861, effective northern leadership simply did not exhibit itself. President-elect Lincoln "sneaked" into the capital and, as Horace Gray learned, "holds his court . . . [at Willard's Hotel which] is full of embryo office-holders. . . . Everybody here seems to look to Lincoln and Lincoln says 'delighted to see you' &c &c., but no one gets his tongue and everyone has his ear." Lame-duck President Buchanan lectured Congress on the incapacity of the national government to restrain the southern states' rash, regrettable, but uncheckable, actions. His recently appointed Attorney General, though staunchly Unionist, privately confided that he "did not think it probable, indeed hardly possible, that Northern officials would still be in the capital on March 4 [1861]." And Buchanan's Secretary of War — *Secretary of War!* — wrote to a Louisiana confidant:

The thought of employing force to oblige a state to remain in the union has never been entertained by the President or any member of his cabinet — He has held, as I do, that it is his duty to protect the public property, in his charge as well as he can — But this principle is virtually an abstraction since with two or three exceptions, the arm[ories] and forts of the U[nited] States have been seized throughout the South. . . . No effort to regain them will be made. . . . The union is passing away like a bank of fog before the wind — But the fate of the South will be that of Sampson — She will pull down the temple, but she will perish amid its ruins.[6]

Little wonder that the North moved sluggishly during the secession winter. Advocates of futility set the cadence. Braver rhythms failed to emerge from the institutions of self-rule — Constitution, political parties, popular conventions — in which since 1776 Americans had taken such pride. On the last unhappy day of 1860, despairing at all he saw and heard from Washington and points farther south, James Russell Lowell asked:

Is it the effect of democracy to make all men cowards? An ounce of pluck just now were worth a king's ransom. There is one comfort, though a shabby one, in the feeling that matters will come to such a pass that courage will be forced upon us, and that when there is no hope left we shall learn a little self-confidence from despair. That in such a crisis the fate of the country should be in the hands of a sneak [Buchanan]! If the Republicans stand firm

---

[6] Wilder Dwight to Horace Gray, February 27, 1861, Horace Gray Papers, Manuscripts Division, Library of Congress (cited hereafter as LC); on the new Attorney General, Edwin M. Stanton, see Charles Sumner to Governor John Andrew, January 28, 1861, John Andrew Papers, Massachusetts Historical Society; War Secretary Joseph Holt to J. O. Harrison, January 14, 1861, J. O. Harrison Papers, LC.

we shall be saved, even at the cost of disunion. If they yield, it is all up with us and with the experiment of democracy.[7]

Southward, in striking contrast to the catatonic quiet along the Potomac, the Confederate States of America formed themselves into a nation in a mood of noisy self-confidence. To add more gall to the North's wounds, it appeared that only secessionists understood how to manipulate successfully democratic machinery and ideas, and for such purposes! By insisting that they were merely exercising the right of revolution, since 1776 sacred to Americans, and by exploiting constitutional conventions in several states to gain their ends, secessionists struck telling blows at northern foes long before Sumter.

Popular conventions were the proudest contribution of Americans to the art of politics and to the practice of democracy. Calhoun had conceived the notion to employ conventions in order to cloak in a democratic mantle the pigmented hold of southern whites on the reins of power. Constructing what Edward Pollard called "one of the most beautiful and ingenious theories in American politics," between 1830 and 1850 Calhoun was able to present as a defense of states' rights his white-rights-only view of a great society. In 1860 his sectional heirs carried theories into practice, while attempts to create acceptable formulae of sectional compromises failed.[8]

While secession conventions moved ahead, would-be peace

---

[7] James Russell Lowell to Charles Nordhoff, in *Letters of James Russell Lowell*, ed. Charles Eliot Norton (New York, 1894), I, 308.

[8] On conventions, the only full study was inspired by the war and Reconstruction, and badly needs redoing: John A. Jameson, *The Constitutional Convention: Its History, Powers, and Modes of Proceeding* (4th ed., Chicago, 1887). The first edition appeared in 1867. On Pollard and many other matters, see Roy F. Nichols, *Blueprints for Leviathan: American Style* (New York, 1963), pp. 134, 143, 130–262 *passim*. For right of revolution, Thomas J. Pressly, "Bullets and Ballots: Lincoln and the 'Right of Revolution,'" *American Historical Review*, LXVII (April, 1962), 647–62.

congresses spent weeks in ultimately vain efforts to create a "compromise of 1860" to take place with earlier sectional treaties of 1820, 1832, 1850, and 1854. "There is no news to write from here [Washington]," Wilder Dwight informed a worried correspondent at the end of February, 1861; "The peace congress came to a dead-lock yesterday. Today they start again. . . . But the peace Congress is a humbug & will I think die a natural death next Saturday unless accidental violence kills it sooner."[9]

All efforts during the secession winter managed only to squeeze out new sell-outs to the South. As voiced by appropriately named Senator Robert Toombs of Georgia, one appealing suggestion took the form of the "Chinese shoe" idea of adding to the Constitution certain unamendable, irrepealable amendments.

The Toombs package called for cementing forever into the national Constitution a provision that laws of the state from which a fugitive fled should determine the criminality of a fugitive. Further, the national Fugitive Slave Law, which had exacerbated northern opinion since 1850, must become even more severe and be strictly enforced in every state, meaning every northern state, of course, without interference from habeas corpus writs or jury trials in state courts, even if states' laws required such procedural niceties. Still further, and forever, congressional laws were to punish in any state anyone "who shall in any manner aid and abet invasion or insurrection in any other State, or commit any other act against the law of Nations, tending to disturb the tranquility of the people or government of any other State."

Obvious paradoxes abounded in this monstrous suggestion as well as in the paler echo which Kentucky's John Crittenden patched up. They issued from self-proclaimed defenders

[9] Wilder Dwight to Horace Gray, February 27, 1861, Gray Papers, LC.

of a state's rights and of limitations on the functions of the national government. Yet, once accepted and enacted, Toombs's proposal would effectively have reduced states to ciphers in the most tender functional arenas that men knew then. In the opinion of John W. Burgess, "To agree to Mr. Toombs's demands, or to Mr. Crittenden's propositions, would have been for the Republicans political and moral suicide."[10]

By early March, 1861, Republican leaders, including Lincoln, were so close to despair as to flirt with such immoral self-destructiveness. The new President in his inaugural address spoke of the proposal for an unamendable amendment favoring slavery: "I understand a proposed amendment to the Constitution — which . . . I have not seen, has passed Congress, to the effect that the federal government, shall never interfere with the domestic institutions of the States, including that of persons held to service. . . . Holding such a provision to now be implied constitutional law [because of Dred Scott], I have no objection to its being made express, and irrevocable."[11]

If the South had called his hand, surely Lincoln would have honored his inaugural promise and exerted his party's weight in favor of the suggested amendment. But mere guarantees forever to transform the national government of the United States into a bodyguard for Negro slavery, with reciprocal diminution of the rights of northern states and of free citizens, proved to be inadequate to checkrein secessionists.

---

[10] John W. Burgess, *The Civil War and the Constitution, 1859–1865* (New York, 1901), I, 99, and see 96–100.

[11] *The Collected Works of Abraham Lincoln*, ed. Roy P. Basler (New Brunswick, N.J., 1953), IV, 270 (hereafter cited as Lincoln, *Works*). But see *ibid.*, 168–69, for a fragment Lincoln set down on the Constitution and the Union. In it, liberty "to all," and the interaction of the Declaration of Independence and the Constitution, received his attention. This is advanced, "radical" thinking for early 1861, which is probably when Lincoln wrote it. How far astray it was from the politically possible then is measurable by comparison with what he said in the inaugural.

Five weeks after Lincoln's inauguration — perhaps the last one ever for an American President — news of Sumter's bombardment levered anger even out of would-be sectional compromisers. Caleb Smith of Lincoln's cabinet so far forgot his Hoosier equanimity as to write: "We must now either vindicate the power of the Government or make an unconditional surrender. We have concluded to test the power of the Government to protect itself."[12]

Brave words, widely echoed. But rhetoric aside, never was a society less well prepared to face challenge. In matters of on-hand or quickly available martial strength the North was fearfully unready to wage even bush-league war, much less the mass conflict which the Civil War unpredictably became. However, obvious modes of effort would improve this deficient condition, and the enemy shared it in any case.

More important by far in 1861 and later was the habit of despair even among Unionists. The North was accustomed to give way. Although the Republican party was at last in the highest office in 1861, it could hardly be said to be in power. Most Republican leaders were anxious to defend themselves as moderates rather than to seek brave new worlds. Across the partisan aisles the Democratic organization lay in apparently unharmonizable factional pieces. Stephen A. Douglas' untimely death robbed the party in Congress of its logical Unionist head and next presidential candidate. As result of the lack of leadership, the Democratic organization accepted guidance from a mixed bag of spokesmen ranging from the Vallandigham depths of malignant covert disloyalty, through Bayard's unending counsels of despair and defeatism, to the staunch Unionism of Andrew Johnson, who soon had to abandon such colleagues in favor of association with the Lincoln party.

---

[12] Caleb Smith to R. W. Thompson, April 16, 1861, Lincoln National Life Foundation.

Limp leaders holding slack reins over a flaccid society formed a weak spring for effective government. Until the war altered matters, most Americans had lived lifetimes without encountering an officer of the national government or even local officials outranking the county's sheriff or city's mayor. "We hardly knew we had a national government except when the quadriennial contest for spoils of office came around," recalled one commentator on the war's significance, and the French observer Count Agenor de Gasparin noted of America: "She is . . . as little governed; above all as little administered, as possible." Save for Negroes, Americans were unaware of restraints, much less accustomed to them.[13] Carlyle is best quoted here; America, he said, is "anarchy plus a street-constable."

The war thrust upon this amorphous society urgent problems of constitutional law about which categories or questions did not exist in the texts, much less solutions. Augmenting armies soon swelled in size to Napoleonic proportions. Internal security needs inspired arrests of civilians by soldiers, habeas corpus writ privilege suspensions, and sporadic censorship of communications media. Subsequently, conscription twisted further the strained political structures that were trying to carry on the snowballing war. Emancipation and the arming of Negroes as soldiers — the equipping of blacks to kill whites — made realities of issues which before Sumter were either nightmares or pipe dreams. And a Reconstruction beyond merely reversing history to 1860 required an assumption of national governmental powers which not even the most outthrust Republicans of 1860 advanced.

To cope with all this the nation had at its disposal a Con-

---

[13] Count Agenor de Gasparin, *America Before Europe*, trans. Mary L. Booth (New York, 1862), p. 338; Edwin Channing Larned, *The Great Conflict, What Has Been Gained, and What Remains to Be Done, Oration, 4th July, Aurora, [Ill.], 1865* (Chicago, 1865), p. 5.

stitution which the great debate of 1860 had disclosed was a source of weakness, not strength. The document was at best irrelevant, quaintly antique, and probably obsolete. The fact that antiwar orators suddenly discovered in the Bill of Rights still another source of inflexible restrictions on national functions, even during wartime, to add to the catalog of limitations already marked out appeared to decrease the utility of the Constitution as a source of power. As example of the apparent inadequacy of the 1787 Constitution to the needs of 1861 and after, its only phrase other than the hazy martial law provision dealing with civil-military relationships was (and is) the prohibition against the quartering of troops in the homes of civilians. This provision tasted more of Tea Party days than of the extensive interventions of uniformed officials into civilian matters, so common after Sumter.

Home-front and occupation-area internal security procedures were no-man's-lands to the tiny professional officer corps, even stranger to uniformed civilians, and most mysterious of all to uninformed jurists. When Sumter was fired on, not one military journal existed to broaden officers' views, a deficiency only partially corrected before late 1862. Law books and journals were mute on civil-military matters. By that time the North's internal security program was lessening in scope and intensity. *Ex parte Merryman* remained only the opinion of Chief Justice Roger B. Taney and was discounted as the unrealistic, Copperhead-colored grumbling of the Dred Scott judge. Until March, 1863, the habeas corpus writ privilege was at the mercy of the predilections of numerous executive officers from Lincoln down. The depth of the Alice-in-Wonderland confusion is evident in this caution from Horace Binney to Francis Lieber, two of the best constitutional lawyers in the United States: "We have talked and written much on the Habeas Corpus question. It is a political rather than a legal question — a mixed political and a legal question.

. . . No one should be dogmatical, or very confident, in such a matter." [14]

Indeed not. The editor of the *American Law Review* complained that "No branch of the law is so badly supplied with literature as that which relates to courts-martials [and trials of civilians by military commissions]. . . . Before the war, all knowledge on the subject of military law had to be derived from . . . bald and inaccurate treatises, from a dozen . . . cases, and from a few official opinions scattered through the volumes of opinions given by the Attorney General, and through orders of the War Department." But this muddle never received much clarification despite Lieber's labors on General Order # 100. [15]

In one illuminating incident on this score, United States Supreme Court Justice David Davis (who was to play a significant role in the Milligan case) received a peremptory summons to appear as a witness in St. Louis at the court martial of an army officer. Indignant, Davis appealed to Judge Advocate General Joseph Holt. "I wish to be advised of my rights and duties touching the whole matter. I am engaged in holding [circuit] courts . . ." Davis complained. "Has the

---

[14] Horace Binney to Francis Lieber, December 23, 1861, printed on unnumbered prefatory page of Binney's *The Privilege of the Writ of Habeas Corpus Under the Constitution* (2d ed., Philadelphia, 1862). The only military precedents were from the essentially dissimilar Mexican War. Soon after that war closed, the highest officers of the Army decided that "no necessity can arise, and no provision need be made by law, to authorize officers of the army to exercise civil functions within the United States in time of peace; nor in time of war can the necessity be so clearly anticipated as to be provided for by law." Senate Executive Document # 5, 31 Cong., 2 sess., p. 3. On the paucity of professional military literature of any sort in 1861–62, see Donald N. Bigelow, *William Conant Church and the Army and Navy Journal* (New York, 1952), pp. 103–5.

[15] *American Law Review*, I (April, 1867), 559–60, in a review of Joseph Holt, *Digest of Opinions of the Judge Advocate General of the Army* (Washington, D.C., 1866).

Court [Martial] . . . a right to take a [civilian] judge from his Court, as a witness — I know nothing, literally, of the Law of Court Martials."[16] Davis was not alone.

Such togetherness in ignorance seriously hindered the precision with which the North came to war and served to impede its course toward a consensus on aims, including a Reconstruction policy. What it boils down to is that before 1861 the American nation and society, save for a corps of southerners headed by Calhoun, had not studied itself. Adverting to this unintrospective tradition, Orestes Brownson judged that "Among nations, no one has more need of knowledge of itself, and no one hitherto had less. It has hardly had a distinct consciousness of its own national existence, and has lived the unreflective life of the child, with no severe trial, till the . . . rebellion, to throw it back on itself and compel it to reflect on its own constitution, its own separate existence, individual tendencies, and ends."[17]

The Civil War forced Americans to study their society, political institutions, and Constitution as never before. Some of Lincoln's contemporaries sensed what scholars until recent-

---

[16] David Davis to Joseph Holt, October 11, 1862, Joseph Holt Papers, L.C.

[17] Orestes Brownson, quoted in John C. Hurd, *The Theory of Our National Existence, as Shown by the Action of the Government of the United States Since 1861* (Boston, 1881), p. vi. Remarkably, an obscure Kentucky lawyer came to this perception earlier than anyone else I find in print. See Robert L. Breck, *The Habeas Corpus and Martial Law* (Cincinnati, 1862), p. 10: "The American people are engaged in a great struggle in the course of which they begin to be, for the first time, thrown upon the serious discussion of the most fundamental and vital principles of enlightened and constitutional liberty. It is an evidence of their past happy exemptions such as those which have rocked other great nations, that these very elementary principles, these rudiments of liberty, are so little known and so feebly apprehended by them. They have lived in the almost unparalleled enjoyment of liberty, but have realized no occasion to study it, and have not analyzed or defined it. They have sailed upon a smooth sea, without the experience of a single

ly failed to see — that great wars are the most intensive social processes men know. The transatlantic commentator Sir James Stephen wrote in 1873 that in the nineteenth century the American Civil War was by far "the [world's] most pointed and instructive modern illustration" of this principle. Who, he asked,

looking at the matter dispassionately, can fail to perceive the vanity & folly of the attempt to decide the question between the North & the South by lawyers' metaphysics about the true nature of sovereignty or by conveyancing subtleties about the meaning of the Constitution and the principles by which the written documents ought to be interpreted? You might as well try to infer the fortunes of a battle from the shape of the firearms. The true question is, what is the real gist & essence of the dispute? What were the two sides really fighting for? [18]

Southerners knew. They were fighting to freeze time at the past, to hold the present, and to prevent change in the future. For them slavery was the war's cause; its retention the war's aim. They enshrined this monolithic goal clearly into the Confederate Constitution beyond the powers of commentators since Alexander Stephens and Jefferson Davis to fudge the matter.

As evidence, consider that the Confederacy's Constitution frankly abandoned the South's pretended devotion to state sovereignty in favor of national, Toombs-like provisions designed perpetually to protect their peculiar institution. In that Constitution slavery was a fixed race relationship which the Confederate national government must enforce against contrary state or local policies wherever the Stars and Bars flew.

Reconstruction in the sense of a return to the Union of the seceded states was unthinkable; a Reconstruction in the con-

---

storm to awaken serious apprehension for their safety, and have never examined the vessel which has borne them, to understand the great timbers and braces that held it together."

[18] Sir James Fitzjames Stephen, *Liberty, Equality, Fraternity* (New York, 1873), pp. 168–69.

text of a reordering of white-Negro relationships toward less than master-servant conditions was criminal.[19]

Not so northward. There, disagreement instead of consensus was the condition on all public matters. Operating with sudden, surprising vigor on all levels of the federal system, political party apparatus offered organized expression to this continuing confrontation throughout the war.

Research has not made clear how political institutions in the northern states withstood the shocks of secession and the unending, accumulating, corrosive strains of war. The fact is that they did. Despite Cassandra cries of doomsayers here and abroad, the political parties remained very much in the business of seeking and controlling the reins of power.

Obviously the political institutions (as distinguished from some antediluvian party leaders) exhibited unanticipated resources of strength and sensitivity. This resiliency and energy are most remarkable with respect to the Democratic organization. Somebody put Humpty Dumpty together again despite the enormous disrupting strains the party suffered out of the Buchanan-Douglas feud and the Republican landslide of 1860. But its disruption, not its reassembly, has received attention. The "Reconstruction" of the Democracy deserves the most serious study and is beginning to receive it.

However it managed the feat, the Democracy rose phoenix-like from these fires. If not purified, it certainly was not petrified. A year after Sumter candidates and platforms under the Democratic label paralleled Republic men and measures right across the state electoral boards that were up that year. By

---

[19] Arthur Bestor, "State Sovereignty and Slavery, a Reinterpretation of Proslavery Constitutional Doctrine, 1846–1860," *Illinois State Historical Society Journal*, LIV (summer, 1961), 174–80, should be contrasted to Charles Lee, Jr., *The Confederate Constitutions* (Chapel Hill, N.C., 1963), and William R. Leslie, "The Confederate Constitution," *Michigan Quarterly Review*, II (1963), 153–65.

1864 Lincoln feared that Democrats would sweep into the White House itself, and soon after Appomattox, having reforged southern links, Democrats were again in a national organization.

Scholarship has done better by the Republicans, perhaps because the Lincoln magnet drew attention there. Like the Democrats the Republican party was plagued by internal strains, but of different sorts. The story is familiar how on highest levels Lincoln managed to wrest leadership from competitors. However, the centering of research on the White House, on a relatively small number of congressional stars, and on a few legislative committees has resulted in an incomplete congressional mosaic. The upshot is that we know far too little of the lineaments of leadership and of policy construction on Capitol Hill. Even more than is true of the Washington story, the states' capitals have remained almost no-historian's-lands in these categories of needed information.

With few exceptions the work of the war-augmented bureaus, departments, and commissions of the national and state governments is still unstudied. The only relatively systematic study of general administrative history now in print almost ignores the war and Reconstruction years. Conscription during the Civil War, a mixed national-state, civil-military process, has not received scholarly attention. We know little about the operation of wartime military elections or of the links which extended from Lincoln's armies to local, state, and national echelons of both parties.

To be sure, better illumination recently has come to hand on the work of such significant ancillary organizations as the Christian Commission and the Sanitary Commission. The first depth penetration is now at hand on the political interaction after Sumter of the Republican organization with prewar abolitionist associations and individuals and with the numerous Protestant church–related charitable and missionary societies. It is now clearer how the North's war to reinstitute the union of states escalated to a far nobler level of abolitionist aspiration. By January, 1863, out of military imperatives primarily but certainly not without the impulsion of augmenting humanitarian and egalitarian motives, Lincoln cast the die in favor of the ending of slavery in the South. Two years later, when Lee surrendered, abolition had become meshed into the developing Reconstruction policy of the Lincoln administration, and nationwide emancipation was under way. By Appomattox, old chimeras of colonization abroad for freedom or of compensation for masters were almost dead.[20]

Even from our deficient knowledge, it is obvious that a good many northern institutions, especially the political ones, obviously enjoyed unanticipated capacities to recruit, to grow, to learn, and to raise sights higher. Was the Constitution as adaptable as the political and administrative institutions to the new needs of war? The intensity and repetitiveness with which Americans asked this question in the months and years after Appomattox astonished commentators here and abroad. The European consensus was that war drums' sounds silenced the operation of all law beyond any need for concern over its nature. Some onlookers derided Americans' Constitution-centeredness as self-idolatry made necessary in absence of a monarch or a state church.

But this concern over the Constitution's condition was not derived from ignorance of national peril. Instead it emerged from widespread and accurate awareness of danger, a growing conviction that the Constitution's fuzziness on fundamental matters required correction. Referring early in 1861 to this sense of the need for constitutional rethinking, Harvard's eminent Busey Professor of Law, Elihu Washburn, told his students that if "our own government . . . is what mod-

---

[20] Reference to almost all these matters is conveniently at hand in the bibliography in James M. McPherson, *The Struggle for Equality: Abolitionists and the Negro in the Civil War and Reconstruction* (Princeton, N.J., 1964), pp. 433–50.

ern theory makes it (i.e., a confederation), [it] is too weak and powerless to stem the current or calm the storm, in which we find ourselves drifting upon the rocks and shoals of hopeless ruin. The relief, if it comes at all, must come from ourselves, from the people . . . or our country is to become the by-word of the pettiest tyrant of the Old World." [21]

Relief did come. After the passage of some time, permissive constitutional interpretations emerged from the White House, from some courts, and from Republican and war Democrat sources on Capitol Hill. Preceding them, and more to Washburn's point, such views flooded in from surprisingly large segments of "the people."

With Sumter, Americans entered on a greater debate than any that had preceded it. In the opinion of one ministerial participant in the unending inquiry, this awareness rose out of widespread realization that "this is the test-hour for all that we have hitherto regarded as fixed and valuable in popular constitutional history, and especially the test-hour of a national government [built] upon the basis of republican freedom."

Theologians, judges, lawyers, legislators, professors, soldiers, businessmen, patriots, and Copperheads saw clearly and swiftly the question the Union must answer in order to survive its test-hour. [22] Was there a way for adequate military strength to amass with which to suppress the rebellion and to keep in check home-front treason and disaffection, without killing the tree of liberty?

The conservative reply was that there was not. Men of this

---

[21] Elihu Washburn, *Lectures Before the Members of the Harvard Law School, January 11, 1861* (Boston, 1861), pp. 19–20.

[22] Rev. Joseph P. Thompson, "The Test-Hour of Popular Liberty and Republican Government," *New Englander*, XXI (April, 1862), 222–23; Joel Parker, *Constitutional Law: With Special Reference to the Present Condition of the United States* (Cambridge, Mass., 1862), pp. 9–10, discusses the increasing number and sharper nature of inquiries into the Constitution since the secession winter a year earlier.

cast of thought took their text from Taney's errant views in the 1861 Merryman case, and holding to such restrictive precepts, rammed them into the defeatist 1864 Democratic platform in such unpalatable form as to inspire repudiation from the party's presidential candidate, George McClellan. By 1868, once again in the Democratic fold, Andrew Johnson helplessly enshrined similar immobilities in his unavailing veto messages and hair-breadth defense in the impeachment.

The alternative northern reply, linked closely to that of Republican party frontrunners, was of a strikingly different character, stressing the release of adequate latent power rather than constraints. "The people have . . . been brought to regard the Constitution . . . as an almost invincible barrier to its [the nation's] acknowledged welfare," wrote a volunteer Army officer in 1861, "and all have set themselves to finding a method by which to overreach it."

But that generation revered written law. Even the Army officer just quoted complained that "we are all trying to elude the Constitution by Constitutional evasions."[23]

Typical of these early "constitutional evasions" was General Benjamin Butler's roundabout way of coping with the shockingly sensitive question of fugitive slaves who entered his lines. Elsewhere, when Generals Charles C. Frémont and David Hunter declared such refugees to be free, they thereby incurred Lincoln's repudiations. The opposite courses of Generals Henry Halleck and George McClellan, who assigned

---

[23] *An Officer in the Field, the Coming Contraband; A Reason Against the Emancipation Proclamation Not Given by Mr. Justice Curtis* [*sic*] (New York, 1862 [reprinted in *Magazine of History*, extra number 49, 1916]), pp. 5–6. The reference to Curtis is to a pamphlet on the indicated subject by Benjamin R. Curtis, *Executive Power* (Boston, 1862), reprinted in George Ticknor Curtis, *Constitutional History of the United States from Their Declaration of Independence to the Close of Their Civil War*, ed. Joseph Culbertson Clayton (New York, 1896), II, 668–86.

units of the United States Army to slave-catching duty, were impossible for Butler to emulate or for most soldiers to stomach. Instead Butler labeled runaway Negroes "contrabands" and with a wink denied altogether that emancipation was involved in his circuitous policy.

A legalistic equivalent to Butler's politic between-lining is evident in an effort by Yale Law Professor Henry Dutton to contradict Taney's restrictive Merryman judgment. It boiled down to an argument that without the Constitution's survival no habeas corpus existed. If Lincoln obeyed the Chief Justice, then the South must win because the North was infested with traitors, as indeed it was.[24] Still, the expediency argument failed to satisfy.

Time had to pass for more comforting concepts to emerge, but, fortunately, not too long a time. By mid-July, 1861, better understanding about the nature of the war was common in the North. Restrained optimism was growing because the political and constitutional institutions northward had not completely collapsed under the shame of secession and the strains of mobilizing its resources. Instead of breakdown the opposite was occurring all around. Vast efforts were assembling men and resources in numbers unknown in the continent's history; home-front treason was going underground out of fear of vigorous punishment. Survival was no longer a daily gamble.[25]

---

[24] Henry Dutton, "Writ of Habeas Corpus; Ex-Parte Merryman" (pamphlet reprint from *American Law Register* [October, 1861], n.p., n.d.). On runaway Negroes and the Army, see Benjamin Quarles, *Lincoln and the Negro* (New York, 1962), p. 68 *et passim*. Note McClellan's plea to S. L. M. Barlow on November 8, 1861: "Help me to dodge the nigger — we want nothing to do with him. . . . To gain that [re-union of states as of 1860] we can not afford to mix up the negro question. It must be incidental and subsidiary. The President is purportedly honest and is really mild on the nigger question." S. L. M. Barlow Papers, Huntington Library.

[25] See Theophilus Parsons, *An Oration Delivered on the 4th of July, 1861, Before the Municipal Authorities of the City of Boston* (Boston,

By a year after Sumter and despite the Bull Run reverse, the Union that was too flaccid in April, 1861, to succor eighty men at Fort Sumter was able almost simultaneously to mount the amphibious expeditions against Richmond, New Orleans, and Forts Henry and Donelson. Something new was abroad in the land. Sober men — even Harvard men — felt inspired by what Charles Francis Adams, Jr., described as "the grandeur of the situation — the dramatic power of the incidents, [and] the Titanic nature of the conflict."

Adams admitted that he found it difficult to specify what energized the impressive spectacle which pleased him, although no one could be "wholly oblivious of it." The passage of time brought sharper awareness. In the words of a Williams College lecturer, "We at the North, all learned that there was in our [Constitution and] Government a power of which we never before dreamed."[26]

In happy reciprocation, popular observation of the strengthening spring of government had bred confidence in the capacity of the Constitution to adapt to any load, strain, or need. "Our Constitution gives us a government second to none in strength," James Russell Lowell exulted in January, 1862. Secession and war had occurred because that strength went unexercised or was diverted into errant channels because of false constitutional conclusions. Now, "with a wisdom and vigor that give every possible presage of success and perpetuity," the Lincoln administration was laboring to restore what the framers of 1787 had built, Lowell wrote.[27]

1861), p. 23 *et passim*, beautifully expresses this widespread sense of renewing confidence.

[26] Charles Francis Adams, Jr., *The Double Anniversary, '76 and '63: Fourth of July Address, Quincy, Massachusetts* (Boston, 1869), pp. 5–6; Charles Demond, *Address Before the Society of the Alumni of Williams College, August 1, 1865* (Boston, 1865), pp. 6–7.

[27] James Russell Lowell, "Loyalty," *North American Review*, XCIV (January, 1862), 159.

Lowell had found a way out of an unpalatable trap of constitutional interpretation, a way which increasing numbers of commentators chose to follow in attempting to gauge the war's unfolding meaning. It was satisfying to applaud the martial and security efforts of the Lincoln administration as necessary and constitutionally proper, at least under the war-power blanket. But it went against the patriot grain to ascribe the existing crisis to the *deficient* handiwork of the men of 1787. "Do we condemn the great constitutional bridge which has carried the nation safe over three-quarters of a century, from beggary to the front rank of the civilized nations?" rhetorically demanded Elizur Wright. "On the contrary, the less we count ourselves its bond-servants, the more we venerate it. It is a most excellent bridge. . . ."[28]

Echoing the theme, Sidney George Fisher, whose contribution to this literature will receive further examination later in this paper, in 1863 set forth the injunction that "we the people of 1862 are not to be commanded to our destruction, by even the best and wisest people of 1787 . . . whose spirits are perhaps now mourning over the destruction of their hopes." He insisted that the Constitution as it stood was fully adequate. Therefore constitutional conventions or amendments were unnecessary to sustain government policies, despite the pleas of

---

[28] Elizur Wright, *The Programme of Peace, by a Democrat of the Old School* (Boston, 1862), pp. 3–4. The American veneration of written law impressed many commentators then and since. Merely as examples see Hermann Eduard Von Holst, *Constitutional and Political History of the United States* (Chicago, 1876–92), I, 68, 75; William Hepworth Dixon, *New America* (London, 1867), II, 294–95: "Whether it be constitutional, general, state, or only municipal, Law is nobly respected by the native American. The Judge of The Supreme Court is treated in Washington with a degree of respect unknown to lawyers in Europe. . . . The State Judges take the place in society held among us by the bishops. Even the village justice, though he is elected by the crowd, is always styled the squire." In Dixon's opinion it was the absence of an established church in America that made its people cling to written law "as to a rock in the midst of a storm."

conservatives toward employment of these mechanisms for defeatist ends looking toward another odious sectional "compromise." In Fisher's view, ". . . nothing remains to be done but to arm the existing Government [and Constitution] by our support, with all the power that a [constitutional] Convention would have, that is to say, with all the whole power of the people."[29]

This concept of the Constitution's adequacy for all purposes and of the Jackson-like primacy of the democratic will was enormously comforting to patriotic penmen. They employed it in a veritable Joseph's coat of variant though conformable imagery. By early 1862 the idea had spread so widely into executive and legislative chambers in Washington and the states — the judiciaries were laggard[30] — into barracks, classrooms, and churches, and into editorial columns and polemical pamphlets, as to warrant description as a consensus.

Many Unionists accepted the adequacy concept and were willing to extend it in the course of events to sanction emancipation. But to men of this cast of thought, the Constitution's heightened powers derived from the emergency of war and

---

[29] Sidney George Fisher, *The Trial of the Constitution* (Philadelphia, 1863), pp. 199–200.

[30] Opposing views in the *Prize Cases*, 2 Black 635 (1863), where Justice Grier accepts the adequacy concept and suggests forcefully how nonsensical it was for the Confederacy to employ all powers but for the Union to deny itself the same privilege. War was war, not an aggravated riot, and a quarter of a million soldiers could not be rationalized into a swollen sheriff's posse. Opposing, Justice Catron wrote privately: "It is idle to disguise the fact that the claim set up to forfeit these ships and cargoes, by the force of a proclamation, is not founded on constitutional power, but on a power assumed to be created by military necessity. Necessity is an old plea — old as the reign of Tibereas; its limits should be looked for in Tacitus. It is the commander's will. The end, we are told, is to crush out the Rebellion; that the whole means are at the Presdt's discretion and that he is the sole judge in the selection of the means to accomplish the end. This is a rejection of the Constitution with its limitations." Justice Catron to J. M. Carlisle, February 26, 1863, in *Legal Historian*, I (1958), 52. I have modernized spelling and omitted italics and unnecessary capitalization.

flowed for war's purposes only. The reunification of the states was the object all sublime, with as little social or economic change as possible from what had been the pattern of 1860. Lincoln was only the most prominent and influential exponent of this view, although he proved to be more educable and mobile than coadjutors of the Blair, Welles, or Bates caliber.

The concept of a Constitution with adequate powers to cope with whatever needs peace imposed as well as with those of war proved to be a wonderfully appealing frontier for exploration by other men who believed that a worthwhile victory in the war could come only by construction of a greater society for a postwar, or other, change. A mobile Constitution, no longer a covenant with the Devil but adequate for God's humanitarian purposes, lured back into major party politics numerous prewar reformers, especially the militant abolitionists. Naturally they chose the Republican camp. Men of this mind became bent on insuring, through politics, that a re–United States never returned to certain conditions as they had been. Again to employ Elizur Wright for a statement on this score, "Such are the general facts that make a restoration of the state [of affairs] before the war equivalent to defeat." Not only reunion and emancipation were needed, Wright continued, but admission to the Constitution's protective provisions of all people heretofore excluded by custom or by contrary national or state laws or judicial decisions.[31]

A concept of constitutional adequacy held by men of such convictions as these synchronized peculiarly well with the fact that from the early days after Sumter, Union troops came into occupation of ever-enlarging parcels of rebel real estate and of numbers of southerners, whites and Negroes. By the end of 1862 the Stars and Stripes flew over northern Virginia and West Virginia, offshore islands and beachheads stretching from the Chesapeake's rim down Florida's Atlantic and Gulf

---

[31] Wright, *op. cit.*, p. 13.

faces, and the augmenting hinterland around New Orleans. Inland, marking the Mississippi's major courses with few rebel interruptions, the Union's armies were valiantly attempting to restore national authority.

These sporadically enlarging, never-contracting enclaves of restored America became stages on which rehearsals took place for some kind of a Reconstruction, or for several kinds. Some of these occupied areas came under charge of mixed military-civil authorities, heavily Protestant missionary–Negrophile in purpose, and dedicated to altering white-Negro relationships in the direction of improvement. Other parcels of conquered Dixie were under the command of Lincoln's novel "military governors," civilians who represented the most extraordinary exertion of national executive authority in American history. Andrew Johnson served as Tennessee's military governor, one of half a dozen such hybrid civil-military appointments.

Other times, or other places in the South, areas were run by military "pros" who cared nothing for "military government" as a "Reconstruction" but who simply did not want to upset anything at all. It was an unsystematic mosaic that developed, and one of Lincoln's purposes in issuing in late 1862 his Emancipation Proclamation, and a year later, in December, 1863, his Reconstruction and Amnesty Proclamation was to provide a degree of order to the Topsy-grown mix.

Whatever the defects of wartime "Reconstruction," the basic fact was that Yankee soldiers consistently held on to conquered zones even if individual battles went awry. The bluecoats' habit of not letting go, displayed across a thousand miles of battlefields, made real by 1862 a question almost unaskable in 1861 — what did America want out of a Reconstruction?[32] This was a question on which spokesmen of the North's

---

[32] Willie Lee Rose, *Rehearsal for Reconstruction: The Port Royal Experiment* (Indianapolis, 1964), is the most complete and almost the only inquiry into the Army's wartime Reconstruction work, and it suffers from its geographical concentration. A full overview is needed. The

never-slumbering democracy were going to be heard. Popular sentiment, largely unconcerned with legalistic metaphysics, was tenaciously aware of the political and constitutional implications of events southward. Emerson offers only one example of commentators who by early 1862 realized that

the war is serving many good purposes. . . . Well, this [is] the task before us, to accept the benefit of the War. . . . It simply demonstrates the rottenness it found. We watch its course as we did the cholera, which goes where predisposition already existed, took only the susceptible, [and] set its seal on every putrid spot. . . . So the War. Anxious [conservative] statesmen try to rule it, to slacken it here and let it rage there . . . to keep the black man out of it; to keep it well in hand. . . . Reconstruction is no longer a matter of doubt. All our action is new and unconstitutional [i.e. unprecedented and extraconstitutional], and necessarily so. . . . Much more in our future action touching peace, any and every arrangement short of forcible subjugation of the rebel country, will be flat disloyalty, on our part. Then how to reconstruct[?] I say, this time, go to work right. Go down to the pan. . . . Leave Slavery out . . . and agree that every man shall have what he honestly earns, and if he is a sane . . . man have an equal voice in the state, and a fair chance in society. . . . This time, no compromises, no concealments. . . .[33]

Republicans naturally seized upon this ready-to-hand battery of assumptions and arguments. Republican radicals in Congress, though a minority within that party, aspired to loft

---

fact was plain that what the Army did in occupied southern areas *was* affecting everything there. As example, note the worried comment to the New York publisher, the conservative Democratic party leader S. L. M. Barlow, from one of his correspondents with the troops, H. D. Bacon, December 4, 1861: "Every step taken in the rebel territory is complicating the necessity for some action to be taken by the Federal authority, as to the disposal of the slaves belonging to the rebels found in arms. . . . I can see how the question will again and again force itself upon the [public's] mind 'Why should the slave property of the rebel be subject to a different military rule than any other [kind] of his property?'" Barlow Papers, Huntington Library.

[33] *Journals of Ralph Waldo Emerson*, ed. Edward Waldo Emerson and Waldo Emerson Forbes (Boston and New York, 1914), IX, 461–65, and see 411–12.

them up to preeminence as war aims. Lincoln employed them to backstop his military government operations and his Emancipation and Reconstruction proclamations. Several examples are clearly documented of the close synchronization between theorizing on the adequacy of the Constitution and political action.

With respect to Lincoln, the most important of these interactions is witnessed in the work and words of the Bostonian, William Whiting. In prewar years Whiting had built up a large reputation as one of the best patent lawyers in the nation. After Stanton and Peter Watson became War Secretary and Assistant Secretary, respectively, they frequently employed Whiting as special War Department counsel. Then, very early in 1863, they brought him into the department as Solicitor. Close friend to Charles Sumner, Henry Wilson, and George Boutwell on Capitol Hill, confidant of Governor John Andrew back in Boston, and admired for his legal acumen by the President and the Secretary of War, Whiting was in an unusually advantageous position to exert influence.

In 1862 he had staunchly supported administration policies in a tract on the *War Powers of the President,* followed with a consideration of *Military Arrests in Time of War.* Applying, after his commissioning, these theoretical arguments to actual wartime problems, Whiting worked out the most incisive depth penetration in print of the adequacy of a President's war-emergency powers in the North but especially in the occupied South.

His preachments were warmly welcomed in the White House as well as in the War Department. In July, 1863, after a series of personal conferences with Lincoln on the Reconstruction question, Whiting set down the sense of his conclusions to the President. They centered on the necessary irreversibility of emancipation, a retrograde possibility which conservatives advocated as a bid to bring the South back in and which men of better moral levels found repellent as a monstrous perversion. But once agreeing that emancipation must hold, the question rose ineluctably concerning the nation's responsibility to the millions of Negroes its needs and powers would free.

Here, Whiting stressed not only the adequacy of the Constitution to cope, but the moral need for coping. The South was conquered territory; the courts had said so and international law repeated the theme. Presidential power offered an obvious way in Whiting's opinion to "keep faith." As Union armies sliced deeper southward,

. . . allow the inhabitants of conquered territory to form themselves into States [Whiting counseled], only by adopting constitutions such as will forever remove all cause of collision with the United States, by excluding slavery therefrom, or continue military government over the conquered district, until there shall appear therein a sufficient number of loyal inhabitants to form a republican government, which, by guaranteeing freedom to all, shall be in accordance with the true spirit of the Constitution of the United States. These safeguards of freedom are required to render permanent the domestic tranquility of the country which the Constitution itself was formed to secure, and which it is the legitimate object of this war to maintain.

Close harmony is evident between Whiting's mid-1863 advices to Lincoln and the President's December, 1863, policy statement on Reconstruction. To be sure, Lincoln chose to pay little attention to the suggestion by Whiting that the "guarantee" clause (Art. IV, sec. 4) formed a bulwark of executive, national war-emergency power. This gambit appealed better to congressional leaders than to the executive.[34]

---

[34] Whiting's wartime writings are assembled in his *War Powers Under the Constitution of the United States. Military Arrests, Reconstruction, and Military Governments* (Boston, 1871), from which (pp. 248–49) the quotation is taken. Chapters, written during the war and as early as 1861 in some instances and issued as pamphlets under several auspices, have variant titles. On Whiting's influence, suggestive evidence is in the Charles Sumner Papers, Houghton Library, Harvard

Consider the periodical piece entitled "The Adequacy of the Constitution," that appeared in January, 1862. Its author was the respected New England jurist and former law partner to Daniel Webster, able, aged Timothy Farrar. In large part his article is a neat restatement of the Marshall-Story tradition of national preexistence, and of the Constitution as supreme law, "not only over the country generally, but in each State particularly." Then Farrar achieved an interpretive salient of greater novelty and large significance. He found in the ignored "guarantee" clause a mandate for national guardianship everywhere, not only in the South, and permanently, not only for wartime and for a brief postwar period, of individual rights against encroachments by states. This guarantee clause, Farrar wrote,

has received [since 1789] no legislative construction, and [has] been furnished with no legislative aid for its administration; but it has a significance not to be overlooked or disregarded. The supremacy of the Nation, and the subordinate responsible position of the States, are ideas inseparable and endlessly involved in this guaranty as to the form of State Governments. . . . The State Governments must not only be preserved in republican form, and defended in the exercise of their appropriate functions by the power of the General Government, according to the guaranty, but they must be held to the actual performance of those functions by the same power, as a necessary condition of the continued existence of the General Government itself. . . . The provisions of the Constitution are the measure of the powers of the Government, and adequate to all the purposes for which it was made. Our fathers made it and put it into successful operation, under circumstances vastly more discouraging than those in which we are now called upon to defend it.[35]

University; the Edwin M. Stanton Papers, LC; the Holt Papers, LC; the Ulysses S. Grant Papers, Southern Illinois University; and the Ethan Allan Hitchcock Papers, Gilcrease Institute. See also Judge Daniel Agnew, *Our National Constitution: Its Adaptation to a State of War or Insurrection* (Philadelphia, 1863).

[35] Timothy Farrar, "The Adequacy of the Constitution," *New Englander*, XXI (January, 1862), 51–73. The quotation is on pp. 70–71.

Within a month after the appearance of this article, Charles Sumner brought to the Senate a resolution to require that Congress should "assume complete jurisdiction" over former rebel regions and establish there "republican forms of government under the Constitution." The time proved to be premature for asserting such legislative national leadership, but not too much so. By July, 1864, in the Wade-Davis bill, Sumner's minority position of 1862 had become the property of a working majority in the Congress. The Wade-Davis bill, as explained by backer Henry Winter Davis, assumed that the guarantee clause

vests in the Congress of the United States a plenary, supreme unlimited political jurisdiction, paramount over courts, subject only to the judgment of the people of the United States, embracing within its scope every legislative measure necessary and proper to make it effectual; and what is necessary and proper the Constitution refers in the first place to our judgment, subject to no revision but that of the people. It recognizes no other tribunal. It recognizes the judgment of no court.[36]

To return to the matter of the work of the "adequacy" school of interpreters, Farrar's influence was direct and significant in providing an underpinning for champions of national, congressional primacy in war and Reconstruction matters. The Philadelphia lawyer, Sidney George Fisher, came to similar conclusions, but he is of larger importance. Fisher provided the first full-scale inquiry into the American Constitution employing views of mid–nineteenth-century European scholarship. Because Fisher was a conservative on race, indeed a Negrophobe, his strongly nationalist conclusions enjoyed the special merit of ostensible objectivity unmarred by the obvious humanitarian penchants of Farrar or Whiting.

---

[36] *Congressional Globe*, 38 Cong., 1 sess., Appendix, 82 (March 22, 1864). See also Charles O. Lerche, Jr., "Congressional Interpretations of the Guarantee of a Republican Form of Government During Reconstruction," *Journal of Southern History*, XV (May, 1949), 192–211.

Fisher started out merely to contradict Horace Binney's 1861 defense of Lincoln's suspensions of the habeas corpus writ privilege, which asserted exclusive executive jurisdiction on this tender matter. But digging made Fisher dig further, and he emerged from his researches at the end of 1862 with the book-length *The Trial of the Constitution*. Like Dicey and Bagehot then, and Woodrow Wilson twenty years later, Fisher condemned the revered but unstudied separation-of-powers and checks-and-balances features of the Constitution, for he found them to be impediments to action. In the English government Fisher discovered a superior model of unitary sensitivity and comforting certainty. By contrast, our Constitution was mechanical, inflexible, and mysterious. Judicial review was no solution, he decided, since by its nature it was ever laggard and because, as in Dred Scott or in the threatening habeas corpus issue, when it acted, it maltreated popular needs. Such rigidity and uncertainty had led to crisis in 1860 and still threatened disaster. The only solution was to accept in Congress "the whole power of the people . . . and the security of the people consists in their control over Congress by the ballot box."[37]

Of course, Whiting, Farrar, and Fisher are not the only "adequacy" writers. But they are the most important ones. They directly influenced the development of policies on both ends of Pennsylvania Avenue. Further, they helped to define clearly public attitudes on the nature and purpose of the Constitution, so that after Appomattox men could come to decisions with little of the somnambulistic flounderings that had blighted useful action during the secession winter.

---

[37] The best biographical data is in William H. Riker, "Sidney George Fisher and the Separation of Powers During the Civil War," *Journal of the History of Ideas*, IV (June, 1945), 397–412. The quotation is on p. 407. Fisher's diary is appearing in successive issues of the *Pennsylvania Magazine of History and Biography*, LXXXVIII and LXXXIX (1964–present).

By the new year 1865 such teachings combined with the Union armies' accelerating successes and in the North inspired a warm flush of optimism. Writing on "Reconstruction," James Russell Lowell spoke of the illuminating glare which the war had cast upon "certain truths" of American life. Most notable was "the amazing strength and no less amazing steadiness of democratic institutions." But now with imminent peace a new test-hour was upon the land; ". . . what are we to do with the country our arms have regained?" Lowell asked. It was common sense, constitutional sense, and justice to enfranchise the freedmen, he concluded prophetically, for "at best, the difficulty, if not settled now, will come up again for settlement hereafter, when it may not be so easy of solution." To be anything less than brave "has the weakness of an expedient which will erelong compel us to reconstruct our reconstruction, and the worse weakness of hypocrisy, which will sooner or later lay us open to the retribution of that eternal sincerity which brings all things at last to the test of its own unswerving standard."[38]

Lincoln had come to the same general conclusion. Speaking publicly on April 11, he adverted to the fact that Grant's "recent successes" had pressed "the re-inaguration of the national authority — reconstruction — which has had a large share of thought from the first . . . much more closely upon our attention." His own plan of December, 1863, was "not the only plan which might possibly be acceptable," Lincoln reminded his audience. For himself, he willingly forwent indulgence in the "merely pernicious abstraction" of theorizing on the condition of the conquered rebel states. Instead he assumed the existence of power for the national government to specify conditions southward. Applauding the provision in Louisiana's new constitution that opened the state's public schools "equally to black and white," the Presi-

---

[38] James Russell Lowell, "Reconstruction," *North American Review*, C (April, 1865), 559, and see 540–59 *passim*.

dent admitted that he wished Louisiana whites would confer the suffrage "on the very intelligent [Negroes], and on those who serve our cause as soldiers."[39]

Three days later Lincoln was dead. To many of his contemporaries and to almost all subsequent commentators, his murder and the news of Lee's capitulation rang down the curtain on the war and brought in another kind of time — the Reconstruction. But Republican frontrunners did not separate the war from the Reconstruction, at least in constitutional terms. Adequacy for the nation's war needs led seamlessly to competency to cope with the needs of the post-battle period that was not quite peace.[40]

The widespread assumption among Republicans of the continuing adequacy of the Constitution to express the dic-

---

[39] Lincoln, *Works*, VIII, 403–5. By 1865, Negro suffrage in the South was such a common-sense solution to the Reconstruction difficulty that objections to the reform appeared foolish to radicals. In England, when reports arrived of Lincoln's jump in racial views, old-line reformer-abolitionist Moncure D. Conway, a Virginia convert to the rights of man, praised the President's advance to the famous historians Carlyle and Froude. Conway recorded that they "urged on me the absurdity of enfranchising the negroes. But, I asked, who else was there in the South to enfranchise?" Moncure Daniel Conway, *Autobiography, Memories, and Experiences* (Boston and New York, 1904), II, 206.

[40] As example, note that Farrar extended his wartime writings and in 1867 published his *Manual of the Constitution of the United States* (Boston, 1867). A summary in John C. Hurd, "Theories of Reconstruction," *American Law Review*, I (January, 1867), 238–64, grew into his *Theory of Our National Existence, op. cit.* The legal profession generally took sides in a debate between Harvard Law School staffers Elihu Washburn, "Reconstruction: The Duty of the Profession to the Times," *Monthly Law Reporter*, XVI (July, 1864), 477–84, and Joel Parker, *Revolution and Reconstruction: Two Lectures Delivered in the Law School of Harvard College, January 1865, and January 1866* (New York, 1866), and *The Three Powers of Government; the Origin of the United States and the Status of the Southern States, on the Suppression of the Rebellion; the Three Dangers of the Republic — Lectures Delivered in the Law School of Harvard College and in Dartmouth College, 1867–68, and '69* (New York, 1869).

tates of the popular voice helps to explain their angry reaction to the obstructive course of Andrew Johnson and to the shockingly unexpected onslaught *by*, not *on*, the judiciary. At the White House and in federal courts especially, conservatives with respect to race and standpatters or would-be reversers of augmenting national functions found welcome to offer such views as constitutional gospel.

For the Alabaman Hilary A. Herbert, who became a prominent legalistic defender of white supremacy, "the only gleam of hope for the Constitution then [1867] was in the Supreme Court." Alexander H. Stephens, the Confederacy's Vice-President and unseated senator-elect from Georgia to the United States, told his state's "Johnson" legislature: "Our only alternative now is, either to give up all hope of constitutional liberty, or to retrace our steps, and to look for its vindication and maintenance in the forums of reason and justice instead of in the arena of arms — in the Courts and in the halls of legislatures. . . ." Echoing the theme, Baltimore attorney and local Democratic partisan Philip C. Friese cautioned jurists that all lawyers would regret it if Congress did not find the Supreme Court in its way.[41]

Perhaps partially in response to many such appeals to its institutional vanity and also to the innate looking-backwardness of legal professionals, by 1866 the Supreme Court shook off its wartime torpor and timidity. The tradition among historians is that congressional radicals, anticipating the judicial drift, in mid-1866 prevented President Johnson from adding more conservatives to the Supreme Court by enacting a law

---

[41] Hilary A. Herbert, *The Supreme Court in Politics; Paper Read Before the Alabama State Bar Association, August 3, 1883* (Montgomery, n.d.), p. 14; Alexander H. Stephens, *Address Before the General Assembly of the State of Georgia, February 22, 1866* (Milledgeville, Ga., 1866), p. 9; Friese, *The Unconstitutionality of Congressional Action: An Essay on the Paramount Unwritten Law* (Baltimore, 1867), p. 26. White supremacy is the "unwritten law" Friese referred to.

holding the tribunal's membership number to seven. But this requires rethinking. Professor Stanley Kutler has shown that President Johnson signed this bill, when he could have easily pocket-vetoed it, and that the jurists themselves, as well as other commentators on the courts, approved of it as a desirable reform.[42]

The point is that the Supreme Court's onslaught of January, 1867, against Republican ways in Reconstruction, was unexpected and thereby the more dismaying. In a sudden display of astonishingly vigorous functional outreaching, the Court belatedly emulated what political institutions had done in 1861. It established new beachheads of judicial review unmatched even by Dred Scott in extent, political significance, and conservatism. Just as 1867 opened, the Court, in the famous Milligan and Test Oath cases, declared unconstitutional the Army's wartime internal security activities which Lincoln had sanctioned in Indiana's critical Copperhead counties, voided a rule requiring lawyers seeking to plead before the Supreme Court to swear first to the past loyalty provisions of Congress' "iron clad test oath," and condemned Missouri's radical-written state constitution which disfranchised and excluded from licensed professions and trades all who could not subscribe a similar state test of past loyalty.

Only twice before, in 1803 and in 1857, had the Court dared to condemn a law of Congress. Both times the jurists had played perilous brinkmanship. Never before had the Court taken a state's constitution — the ultimate *vox populi* — under review. By the Milligan and Test Oath decisions the Court was engaged in a most radical enlargement of the power of a

---

[42] Stanley Kutler, "Reconstruction and the Supreme Court: The Numbers Game Reconsidered," *Journal of Southern History,* XXXII (February, 1966), 42–58. "There seems to have been no opposition to the law," editorialized the *American Law Review,* "which was in no sense a political measure, however much political feelings may have aided in its passage." I (October, 1866), 207–8.

branch of the central government, equal to that which Johnson assumed with respect to the executive's capacity to re-
build during "peacetime" the South's state governments.

Antitotalitarian predilections of the twentieth century
against military rule over civilians and against loyalty oaths
have overlaid these decisions with a patina of liberalism which
they have never deserved, save rhetorically and when excised
from their contexts. In 1867 radical Republicans understood
that liberalism was Negro-centered. The civil liberties the
Court defended in the Milligan and the lawyer's Test Oath
cases were those of ex-rebels and recent traitors, white men
exclusively. There were other Americans then, after all.[43]

There were Negroes. The radical Republican consensus
was that the war-strengthened spring of national government
must guard the ennobled level of civil and political rights,
especially of freedmen, against infringement by and in the
states. Republicans feared the revival of a states'-rights sentiment, and not without reason. Ready to the Republicans'
hands were the weapons which they had discovered soon
after Sumter that substantiated national, congressional primacy in Reconstruction. Chief among these comforting tools
was the "guarantee clause." Some front-runners such as Sumner and John Norton Pomeroy insisted also that the Declaration of Independence and the Bill of Rights were merged into
the body of the Constitution through the Fifth and Fourteenth amendments as negative limitations on the nation and
the states in the old sense of a bill of wrongs, and as positive
goals which all American governments must protect.[44]

---

[43] See the treatment in Benjamin P. Thomas and Harold M. Hyman,
Stanton: The Life and Times of Lincoln's Secretary of War (New York,
1962).

[44] On the Fourteenth Amendment concept, see John Norton Pomeroy, *An Introduction to the Constitutional Law of the United States*
(New York, 1868), pp. 149–52; Boston *Commonwealth*, January 27,
1866; Alfred H. Kelly, "The Congressional Controversy over School
Segregation, 1867–1875," *American Historical Review*, LXIV (April,

Of course not all reformers concentrated attention on the South or on Negroes.[45] Ignoble as well as sincere persons exploited the opportunities for realizing aspirations which the war and Reconstuction had opened. However, the concept of constitutional adequacy for any ends that political institutions demanded was a common denominator, whatever the goal or the motivation. Optimism was the pervasive characteristic of almost all constitutional views other than the conservative, a spirit well illustrated by Charles Francis Adams, Jr., who in 1870 met an Illinois legislator fresh from the enactment of the so-called "Granger" state constitution. It required Illinois to establish by law a regulatory commission to set railroad and grain warehouse rates. Adams expressed doubt that such legislation would successfully overcome the difficulties which swollen corporate structures were causing in states. Indignant at the suggestion, the Illinoisan replied: "Difficult! Why, I don't think I should have any trouble in drawing up an act in half an hour which would settle the whole thing."[46]

We are still trying to "settle the whole thing" for which the over-optimistic Illini allotted a half-hour a century ago. Enjoying the insight that hindsight affords, we know that neither the radical Republicans nor the Illinois Grangers were to succeed in any total sense. But the men of the sixties lacked prescience. They stumbled as trailblazers must, in search of shores dimly seen. Optimistically blundering ahead, Republican radicals made great progress in gaining abolitionist and

---

1959), 537–63; Charles E. Larsen, "Nationalism and States' Rights in Commentaries on the Constitution After the Civil War," *American Journal of Legal History*, III (1959), 360–69.

[45] Henry Villard offers a convenient catalog of reforms other than those centering on the South and on Negroes, in *Journal of Social Science*, II (1870), 202–13.

[46] Charles Francis Adams, Jr., *Remarks . . . on the Subject of a National Rail Road Commission, Before the Merchants' Association of Boston . . . February 25, 1882* (Boston, 1882), p. 4.

Unionist ends. They failed to gain for freedmen permanent post-emancipation political and civil equality. Worse, as time passed, they stopped caring that they had not won earlier goals. Three-quarters of a century slipped by as in courts and legislatures champions of constitutional limitations took the lead, and the commitments to equality that Americans had entered into during the wartime and post-Appomattox Reconstruction remained deferred.

Today these commitments once more impact loudly on the moral sense of the nation. Constitutional concepts and political attitudes analogous to those of the Civil War and Reconstruction scene are again current. One can hope that when a century hence historians come to evaluate our time, they will give it as good a report as the young French journalist Georges Clemenceau felt able to send from Washington in 1865: "The events of the last four years have taught me never to give up hope for this country."[47]

---

[47] Georges Clemenceau, *American Reconstruction, 1865–1870*, ed Fernand Baldensperger (New York, 1928), p. 41.

Comment on
Harold M. Hyman's Paper

ALFRED H. KELLY
Wayne State University

First let me say a word or so concerning the extraordinary revolution in the historiography of the Civil War and Reconstruction which is implicit in Professor Hyman's thoughtful, excellent, and creative paper. This revolution, of course, did not begin with him; it has been foreshadowed in the writings of C. Vann Woodward, Eric L. McKitrick, James M. McPherson, Ralph Korngold, and John Hope Franklin, to mention only a few. Yet for a historian who was nurtured upon the dicta of Avery Craven, James G. Randall, Claude Bowers, and George Fort Milton, as well as the earlier writings of Howard K. Beale, and who also recalls the point of view implicit in T. Harry Williams, David Potter, and the early Kenneth Stampp, the revolution is too extraordinary to be passed over in silence. Professor Hyman's outlook, it seems to me, represents a kind of consummation of the whole recent revolutionary process in the historiography of the war and Reconstruction. Implicitly, if not explicitly, he sees the war very much as James Russell

Lowell and E. L. Godkin saw it a hundred years ago. The historiography of the 1930's, accordingly, has simply been quietly junked.

Professor Hyman accomplishes this, like other recent contemporary writers on the Civil War and Reconstruction, mainly by altering the premises upon which his analysis rests. For Professor Hyman southern rupture of the Union becomes a deliberate attempt to preserve a way of life at once obsolete and morally evil, so that the Republican refusal to conciliate the South on slavery and secession becomes patriotic and enlightened public policy rather than something corrupt, stupid, or benighted. In the same fashion, by silently altering two or three premises underlying his approach to Reconstruction — upon the validity of states' rights and strict constructionist constitutional doctrine, upon the desirability of strong federal action in the field of civil rights, and above all, upon the fundamental nature of Negro-white relations in the South — he relegates the older historiography of Reconstruction to the historians' boneyard.

The technique reminds me a little of that which Machiavelli used to destroy the political metaphysics of the late Middle Ages with respect to sovereignty, the church, and the Holy Roman Empire. The Florentine historian, you will recall, simply started from new premises about the nature of politics and power and at one stroke thereby rendered obsolete nearly all prior theory upon church and state. He did not attack earlier doctrine; he simply ignored it. So, also, with Professor Hyman.

The foregoing amounts to little more than a light-hearted preliminary observation. Let me turn now in somewhat more detail to the ideas in the realm of constitutional history which Professor Hyman presents. One which gives me just a little pause is his argument that the Constitution in 1860 was "a source of weakness, not strength," that it was "at best irrelevant, quaintly antique, and probably obsolete. The fact that antiwar orators suddenly discovered in the Bill of Rights still another source of inflexible restrictions on national functions, even in wartime . . . appeared to decrease the utility of the Constitution as a source of power." E. L. Godkin is quoted at the beginning of his paper, you will recall, to much the same effect — the Constitution as it stood in 1860 was "provisional, experimental, defective," and made possible the "strains set up by the champions of slavery's extension" in the generation before the war.

In one sense, one cannot help but agree, and yet this interpretation, it seems to me, concedes just a little too much to the validity of the various southern and states' rights constitutional doctrines of a century ago. One need not go over to an extreme Crosskey interpretation of pre–Civil War American constitutional history to read the matter quite differently.[1] A modified nationalist construction of these years, such as that presented thirty years ago by A. C. McLaughlin, points out that beginning in 1787 the Constitutional Convention, the authors of the *Federalist Papers*, successive early Congresses, and finally the Supreme Court of the United States worked out a metaphysics of national sovereignty entirely adequate to serve the purposes of an increasingly united nation. Even the Jeffersonians, with some inconsistencies, accepted this metaphysics after they came to power — witness the purchase of Louisiana and Joseph Story's conversion to Hamiltonian nationalism.[2]

Between 1815 and 1840, however, American constitutional doctrine became increasingly trifurcated, developing three

---

[1] William W. Crosskey, *Politics and the Constitution in the History of the United States* (Chicago, 1953), argues that the constitutional fathers actually intended virtually to establish a unitary state. By this interpretation, even John Marshall later "subverted" somewhat the true intent of the Constitutional Convention of 1787.

[2] A. C. McLaughlin, *A Constitutional History of the United States* (New York, 1935). This is the classic "nationalist" approach to pre–Civil War constitutional history.

main streams which flowed alongside one another — often in conflict, but without any one of them entirely overwhelming the other two. The oldest of these — and ultimately the most viable and useful to national sovereignty — was that of the Convention nationalists, which flowed on into the Hamiltonian-Marshall doctrines of national sovereignty, national supremacy, and broad construction. However, Hamiltonian nationalism after 1815 or 1820 found itself increasingly driven into the sanctuary of the Supreme Court of the United States. But the Court itself never faltered — well, hardly ever, to borrow a phrase from Gilbert and Sullivan. Even Taney's Court continued to administer the corpus of constitutional law in a thoroughly nationalistic fashion, as Carl Brent, C. B. Swisher, and B. F. Wright made clear some years ago.[3] The much maligned Dred Scott opinion, by the way, is a thoroughly nationalistic assertion of federal constitutional supremacy; it musters the Bill of Rights and not state sovereignty doctrine in defense of slavery in the territories.[4]

It was this nationalistic body of doctrine — not quaint, not obsolete, but still very much alive even if driven into the sanctuary of the Court and portions of the Republican party — which Lincoln invoked in his First Inaugural and which he resorted to in order to save the Union after the call to arms. What happened, I would argue, was not the birth of a new

---

[3] C. B. Swisher, *American Constitutional Development* (Cambridge, Mass., 1943, 1954); B. F. Wright, *The Growth of American Constitutional Law* (Boston, 1942).

[4] For example, Taney's comment in Dred Scott that the United States "is sovereign and supreme in its appropriate sphere of action," and his nationalistic interpretation of the Constitution's citizenship clause, 19 Howard 393 (1857), 401, 406 ff. Taney's most powerful exposition of national sovereignty and national judicial ascendancy appears in *Ableman v. Booth*, 21 Howard 506 (1859): "It was felt by the statemen who framed the Constitution that . . . in the sphere of action assigned to it [the "general government"], it should be supreme and strong enough to execute its own laws by its own tribunals, without interruption from state authorities."

wartime Constitution, but the resuscitation of an old one, at least in the metaphysical sense. It is doubtful that even the imperatives of war could have rescued the country from the constitutional paralysis of 1860–61, had not Lincoln and his principal advisors understood quite thoroughly the old Hamiltonian-Marshall-Webster-Story doctrine and been prepared to put it immediately to work.

The emergence of a second major constitutional stream — that of the state sovereignty doctrines of John C. Calhoun, as set forth in the *South Carolina Exposition and Protest*, the *Fort Hill Address*,[5] and the subsequent pronunciamentos of Calhoun and other southern constitutional theorists — is only too well known to all the historians present here. It is important to realize, however, as Professor Hyman makes clear, that Calhoun's state sovereignty doctrines had little or nothing to do with the paralysis of national will which overtook the North for a time in 1860 and 1861. Calhoun's ideas served as a metaphysics to justify southern destruction of the Union, but they had no relevance whatever to the North's constitutional dilemma. Even the southern states recognized, as Professor Hyman points out, that Calhoun's doctrines were of no real value in the creation of a viable southern federal constitutional republic. They were quietly abandoned, first at Montgomery and then at Richmond, already having served their disruptive purpose.

It was the third major constitutional stream, swelling and growing after 1815 — that of states' rights, strict construction, and that most invidious and neglected offspring of the foregoing two, the doctrine of dual federalism — which in the crisis of 1860–61 did so much damage to northern will and

---

[5] *Works of John C. Calhoun*, ed. Richard K. Cralle (New York, 1854, 1957), VI, 1–57, 59–123, respectively. On Calhoun's theories see C. M. Wiltse, "Calhoun's Democracy," *Journal of Politics*, III (May, 1941), 210–23.

purpose and which indeed very nearly deprived the republic of the rational means to defend itself.

States' rights doctrine, which paradoxically had been sheltered in the house of the northern Democratic party, had by 1860 accomplished three horrendous results, all of them tending to the destruction of effective national government. First, its metaphysics of extreme strict construction of federal powers — a metaphysics which began with Jefferson's bank paper of 1791 and which found further sanctification in Madison's internal improvements veto of 1817,[6] in Jackson's Maysville veto[7] and antibank messages, and in Democratic party tariff theory — succeeded in very nearly destroying entirely the old Federalist bureacratic mechanism as an instrument of national sovereignty.

If anyone wishes firsthand documentary evidence of how far this erosion of pragmatic national authority had proceeded between 1815 and 1860, let him turn to the dusty pages of Richardson's papers of the presidents, and peruse the annual messages to Congress of Fillmore, Pierce, and Buchanan. They reveal an extraordinarily calm acceptance of something amounting very nearly to total destruction of the federal governmental mechanism except in foreign affairs, minimal public works, and a little frontier Indian fighting.[8] It was this

---

[6] In vetoing the Internal Improvements bill of 1817, Madison objected that the measure in question "would have the effect of subjecting both the constitution and laws of the several states in all cases not specifically exempted to be superseded by laws of Congress. . . ." *Messages and Papers of the Presidents*, comp. James D. Richardson, I, 570. Thus, the same Madison who had objected successfully to the inclusion of the word "specifically" in the Tenth Amendment in 1789 in effect wrote it in now.

[7] *Ibid.*, II, 1046.

[8] See, for example, Fillmore's annual message of December, 1851, which confines federal concerns to foreign affairs, exports, federal finance, Indian hostilities, the post office, rivers and harbors, and one or two other minor matters. *Ibid.*, III, 2659. Pierce, in his annual message of December, 1853, observed that "vast as are the functions and duties

situation which gave point to the observation by Count de
Gasparin which Professor Hyman quotes, that American were
"as little governed; above all as little administered as possible." It was this erosion of the Hamiltonian tradition of
positive national government which by 1860 had almost completely destroyed the federal bureaucratic mechanism and so
deprived the executive of the pragmatic means to deal with a
large-scale insurrection against national sovereignty.

States' rights doctrine had a second horrendous result inimical to national survival: it spawned the corollary doctrine of
dual federalism, a constitutional concept far more deadly in
its consequences for adequate federal sovereignty than anything Calhoun had ever had to say. For Calhoun's ideas, as
already observed, were simply irrelevant to the political and
legal processes of the federal government, but dual federalism, by contrast, effectively tied Buchanan's hands.

Briefly, dual federalism was the doctrine — which, irony of
ironies, the old nationalist James Madison had first expounded
effectively — which held that national and state sovereignty
were in a manner of speaking twin sisters, operating alongside
one another on a single plane of total equality, neither superior to the other and each totally efficacious in her own sphere.
Under this doctrine, federal sovereignty, far from being ful-
filled at the expense of the states when necessary, as the old
Hamiltonian-Marshall doctrine of national supremacy had it,
could move only in an autonomous area of its own, totally

---

of the Federal Government . . . yet the substantive power, the popular force, and the large capacities for social and material development
exist in the respective states, which, all being of themselves well constituted republics, as they preceded, so they alone are capable of maintaining and perpetuating the American Union." *Ibid.*, p. 2746. And
Buchanan, in his inaugural, described the federal Constitution as "a
grant from the States to Congress of certain specific powers," and he
added that "long experience and observation have convinced me that
a strict constriction of the powers of government is the only true, as
well as the only safe, theory of the Constitution." *Ibid.*, p. 2965.

isolated from contact with the immediate functions of the states.

It was this metaphysics of coequal federal and state sovereignty which enabled Buchanan with perfect seriousness to enunciate the constitutional absurdity that secession was "neither more nor less than revolution," since the Union was intended to be perpetual, but that the federal government was without power to move against its sister sovereigns, the several states, even though the agents of the latter might engage in a grossly disruptive violation of the Union itself.[9] Even the Civil War did not extinguish entirely this constitutional solecism. It lived on to reassert itself in *United States* v. *Knight*, in the First and Second Child Labor cases, in *United States* v. *Butler*, and in *Carter* v. *Carter Coal Company*, finally to be done to death in the great Court crisis of 1937 and the limited constitutional revolution that followed.

A close corollary of the doctrines of strict construction and dual federalism was that of limited executive prerogative. The progressive destruction of the pragmatic area of federal sovereignty accomplished by strict construction created a situation in which there was little or nothing outside the realm of foreign affairs over which the President could preside. Without a working federal bureaucratic mechanism, it was not only easy but practical to accept the old myths inherited from the revolutionary era that executive prerogative was somehow inimical to democracy and that legislatures alone could act to fulfill the popular will. Washington, Jefferson, and Jackson had been positive instruments of national sovereignty; by contrast, Pierce and Buchanan became glorified chief clerks. Here, again, was a concept of office and power which nearly destroyed the Union. It helped paralyze Buchanan in 1860 and had to be swept into the discard before Lincoln could act

---

[9] *Ibid.*, V, 3165–67.

effectively.[10] *In short, if it was Calhoun's Constitution, so-called, that produced secession, it was Buchanan's that produced national paralysis.*

What happened after 1861, I would argue, was a tremendous revival of the old nationalist doctrines, both with respect to federal-state relations and with respect to executive prerogative. The precedents were there in ample numbers to do the job — Washington's action with congressional sanction in the suppression of the Whiskey Rebellion, the Jacksonian assertion of presidential capacity to deal with nullification and potential insurrection, the Force Act of 1833, and finally the repeated assertions of national sovereignty, national supremacy, and broad construction by the Supreme Court of the United States — the doctrines of John Marshall, nay even of Roger B. Taney himself. The important point, it seems to me, is that the old Federalist-Whiggish Constitution was still there, even if buried under thirty years of dust and disuse outside the halls of the judiciary, and in the hands of an old Henry Clay Whig and his executive and congressional associates it took on an astonishing vigor in a very short time.

Now this distinction between Professor Hyman's doctrine of a new war Constitution and the idea of the revival of an older Hamiltonian-Marshall Constitution may seem to you to be rather academic and picayunish, but I have drawn it for a very fundamental reason — it seems to me to be extremely significant that the people of the North, almost without excep-

---

[10] It was Buchanan's *fainéant* theory of executive power as much as his notions of dual federalism and strict construction that paralyzed him in the secession crisis. In his annual message in December he insisted that "Apart from the execution of the laws, as far as this may be practicable; the Executive has no authority to decide what shall be the relations between the Federal Government and South Carolina. . . . Any attempt to do this . . . would be a naked act of usurpation." *Ibid.*, p. 3166. Lincoln, needless to say, acted upon a radically different theory of the executive prerogative. See E. S. Corwin, *The President: Office and Powers* (New York, 1948), pp. 279–81, 484–86.

tion, after 1861 maintained the idea of the war as prosecuted under a rationale of constitutionalism and constitutional continuity rather than under a rationale of Rousseauean revolutionary doctrine and some concept of federal sovereignty as sanctioned by a mass "will of all." For, as I shall attempt to argue, it was the predominance of the doctrine of constitutional continuity, as against a Rousseauean or even Jeffersonian notion of revolution throughout the war, which set up the basic constitutional dilemma that was to characterize the Reconstruction era.

This assumption of constitutional continuity is, in fact, implicit in the central thesis of Professor Hyman's paper, which, I take it, is that the war Constitution became the basis for the formulation of postwar congressional Reconstruction theory and that the basic radical congressional ideas about Reconstruction evolved during the war and not after 1865. Professor Hyman documents very beautifully the emergence of an "adequacy theory" in the North, with respect both to war and Reconstruction — the thesis that the Constitution as now perceived was adequate not only for the prosecution of the war but also for the exigencies of the restoration of the southern states to the Union and the decisive solution of the Negro problem. The Boston lawyer William Whiting, he makes clear, worked out the "conquered provinces theory" of the relationship of the federal government to the southern states as early as 1863, which is well before Thaddeus Stevens sounded the same theme on the floor of the House of Representatives. And it was Timothy Farrar, old Whig nationalist, who worked out the constitutional doctrines under which Congress presently enacted the Wade-Davis bill — which was to be so useful to the radicals — that Congress had the power to act under the guarantee clause of Article IV of the old Constitution.

But all of these arguments are "conservative" in a fundamental sense. That is, they assume that the "old Constitution," properly interpreted, provided the national government with an adequate legal foundation both for the prosecution of the war and for postwar Reconstruction. With the possible exception of Fisher, all appeal deliberately to the Hamiltonian-Marshall tradition of national sovereignty and national supremacy. Farrar, for example, relies heavily upon Marshall's opinions in *McCulloch* v. *Maryland* and *Martin* v. *Hunter's Lessee* to establish the orthodoxy of his constitutional doctrines. And his argument has an almost Crosskey flavor to it: the Constitution, thoroughly nationalist in original intent, had been subverted from the beginning by the same class of politicians "that had objected to its acceptance."[11] The "true" Constitution therefore must now be recovered.

Sidney George Fisher's work, it must be admitted, has in part a different flavor, for it contains an attack on the idea of constitutional government within limits fixed by judicial review in the American tradition. But Fisher is not really a constitutional radical; rather, he wants an evolving constitutional system after the British parliamentary tradition, so that Congress rather than the Supreme Court is to become the custodian of constitutional orthodoxy. This argument may sound fairly radical today, but to a generation accustomed to Jefferson's and Jackson's arguments against judicial ascendancy, it was not necessarily that at all.[12]

In short, the war generated a revival of broad Hamiltonian constitutional doctrine, but it did not at all break down constitutionalism itself or replace it with a psychology of "revo-

---

[11] Timothy Farrar, "The Adequacy of the Constitution," *New Englander*, XXI (January, 1862), 51 ff.

[12] "The legislature," Fisher argues, "makes laws and represents the people; it is therefore supreme." But he remains a constitutionalist to the core; after deriving congressional ascendancy from the Constitution itself, he asserts, "It thus would appear that our Constitution, actually, does what it was intended to do, create a government adequate to the exigencies of the Union." *The Trial of the Constitution* (Philadelphia, 1863), pp. 60, 142.

lutionary legitimacy." The war presently became a crusade against slavery, but the crusade, as carried on both by the President and Congress, stayed within the tradition of constitutional forms. The Emancipation Proclamation, for example, pretends to rest strictly upon a constitutional base, while Lincoln's veto of the Wade-Davis bill was taken in considerable part because he "doubted the competence of Congress to act" in its pretended emancipation of all southern slaves.[13] And that veto, in spite of the Wade-Davis manifesto, in fact converted the Republican party to the necessity of emancipation by constitutional amendment, as the Constitutional Union party platform[14] and the subsequent adoption by Congress of the Thirteenth Amendment make clear.

This concept of constitutional continuity and of reform within the limits of constitutional orthodoxy, I would argue, carried over into the Reconstruction era, where the great majority of the so-called Republican radicals in fact subscribed to a constitutionalists' approach to both the southern and Negro problems. To me, this is a fact of immense significance. Too often the quarrel between Johnson and Congress, in the old constitutional history, at least, was presented as a controversy between constitutionalists and revolutionists, a struggle between the advocates of constitutional legitimacy and a radical revolutionary party intent upon establishing a revolutionary military republic. The fact is that it was nothing of the sort — it was instead a continuation of the old prewar dispute between state sovereignty and dual federalism, and Hamiltonian nationalism. The triumph by the Congressional radicals in 1866 and 1867, with the enactment of the Civil Rights Act, the passage of the Fourteenth Amendment through the two houses, and the subsequent adoption of the

---

[13] James G. Randall and Richard N. Current, *Lincoln, the President: The Last Full Measure* (New York, 1955), p. 194.

[14] Edward Stanwood, *A History of the Presidency, from 1788 to 1897* (Boston, 1924), p. 302.

Congressional Reconstruction program, in no sense spelled the triumph of revolutionary legitimacy. No one can read the debates of 1866 to 1868 in the *Globe* without being forcibly impressed with the fact that the overwhelming number of so-called Radical Reconstruction leaders — Bingham, Boutwell, Trumbull, Conkling, Fessenden, Sherman, Wilson, Howard, Morrill, and others — staged their arguments within an essentially conservative constitutional frame.

Thus Trumbull's defense of the Civil Rights bill, for example, was based upon his argument for the existence of a so-called "old" Bill of Rights binding the states in the so-called comity clause of Article IV of the old Constitution and upon his argument that Congress could enact legislation endowing the freed man with civil rights pursuant to its authority to implement the newly adopted Thirteenth Amendment.[15] And Bingham, the historians present will recall, forced the amendment of Trumbull's bill on the floor of the House to strike out a sweeping "no discrimination" clause because he believed Congress, without benefit of a constitutional amendment, had no power to enact such a provision.[16] And so on.

The fact of the essentially conservative constitutional orientation of the congressional radicals has been too often obscured; they have been represented instead as engaged in something closely resembling the actions of the French convention of 1793 or of Cromwell's dictatorship. That on occasion elements essentially revolutionary crept into radical psychology and even statutory enactment is to be admitted. The contradictory provision with respect to the requirement imposed on the southern states in the ratification of the Four-

---

[15] See, for example, Trumbull's careful exposition of the significance of *Corfield* v. *Coryell*, 6 *Fed. Cas.*, 546 (1823), as establishing the constitutional foundation for congressional action to protect civil rights under Article IV of the "old Constitution." *Congressional Globe*, 39 Cong., 1 sess., pp. 474–75.

[16] *Ibid.*, p. 1291.

teenth Amendment came close to being such; perhaps, also, so did the provision for military trials in the Civil Rights Act of 1866[17] and Freedmen's Bureau bills, although these latter provisions were conceived as essentially emergency war measures rather than permanent parts of a restored constitutional system.

But the argument, presented in its classic form in Beale's *Critical Year*,[18] that the radicals in 1866 stood poised on the edge of the creation of a revolutionary unitary republic is, I believe, essentially false. They were nowhere near it. They merely wanted to use a Hamiltonian concept of a war Constitution to clean up what they regarded as an emergency postwar situation. Further than that they did not propose to go. Even the view of Johnson's impeachment as essentially a revolutionary act tending to the establishment of a revolutionary parliamentary government is, I would argue, essentially false. It neglects the general consensus that the radicals, and indeed most Americans of the time, had developed with respect to Johnson — that he was a drunkard and a madman. His impeachment, in short, was in the Pickering tradition, not in any revolutionary tradition of the 1793 French convention and the "will of all," in spite of Ben Butler's eleventh article in the bill of particulars.

Now if we accept the fact that the so-called radicals were, after all, constitutionalists, we have some insight into the ultimate failure of their program. For the constitutional frame within which they operated confronted them with three constitutional dilemmas, only one of which they were able to overcome successfully. The other two defeated them — at least with respect to the professed program for the Negro.

The constitutional obstacle they successfully overcame was

---

[17] 14 *U.S. Statutes at Large* 27 (1866).
[18] Howard K. Beale, *The Critical Year: A Study of Andrew Johnson and Reconstruction* (New York, 1930).

that of the separation of powers — the independent constitutional authority and limitations which the President and the Court imposed on the radical program. They curbed Johnson by means entirely constitutional — simply by winning an overwhelming victory in the congressional election of 1866. The impeachment, by the way, was an act of angered outrage in relation to the Stanton removal, not something essential to the integrity of the radical program.

The Court basically curbed itself by acting within the same constitutional tradition as Congress. I would disagree a little, I think, with Professor Hyman's argument that the Court's position was completely reactionary. It was a court, after all, controlled largely by Lincoln appointees, who were deeply and genuinely concerned with the problem of civil liberties.[19] And if the Milligan opinion seems rather too reactionary in terms of the northern war problem, it must be remembered that the judges did not save Milligan from a well-deserved hangman's noose [20] until the war was safely out of the way. As for the Cummings and Garland cases, there is a good deal to say for the Court's repudiation of *ex post facto* exculpatory oaths — I recall a fine book of a few years ago by Professor Hyman, casting rather stern aspersions on the very idea of exculpatory oaths as constitutionally dubious, politically inefficacious, and morally wrong.[21] The Court's final position on Reconstruction, in fact, was taken within a year or so, in *Texas v. White*,[22] in which the justices virtually made peace with the radical program — which they comprised with little or no difficulty within orthodox constitutional law.

---

[19] David M. Silver, *Lincoln's Supreme Court* (Urbana, 1956), pp. 210 ff.

[20] Corwin, *op. cit.*, p. 369. The "constitutional corrective," Corwin aptly reveals, was applied "after the war was safely over."

[21] Harold Hyman, *To Try Men's Souls: Loyalty Tests in American History* (Berkeley, Calif., 1959).

[22] *Wallace* 700 (1869).

Ultimately two other constitutional barriers defeated the radicals — barriers which posed dilemmas to the Republican radicals precisely because they were constitutionalists. The first of these was the limitation imposed by the essentially federal character of the American constitutional system, which at last made it impossible to set up a comprehensive and unlimited program for the integration of the Negro into the southern social order. Such a program could have been effected only by a revolutionary destruction of the states and the substitution of a unitary constitutional system, and the constitutional conservatism of the radicals made that impossible. In spite of Mr. Beale, they did not seriously consider this possibility. Instead their resort to the Dead States theory in 1866–67 was precisely a *Reconstruction* device — that is, a device not for destroying the old system of state-federal relations but for reintroducing the southern states into the federal system. This they completed, in legal terms, within two or three years of the time they destroyed the Johnson governments, and one peruses private papers and the pages of the *Globe*, in vain, I would argue, for any serious evidence that they ever intended to do anything else.

But the commitment to traditional state-federal relations meant that the radical Negro reform program could be only a very limited one. Basically the Fourteenth and Fifteenth amendments constituted attempts to impose certain guarantees, at least of a political kind, upon the southern states within the framework of traditional federalism, for the civil and political rights of the Negro. Granted the willingness of the great majority of white southerners to take advantage of the limitations of the federal system to subvert those guarantees, however, the failure of such a program was an almost foregone conclusion.

So, also, the Ku Klux Klan Act[23] and other measures like it

---

[23] 17 *U.S. Statutes at Large* 13 (1871).

were but feeble instruments for the protection of Negro civil rights within the southern states, for the federal system meant that the core crimes against Negroes were not even brought under indictment, while local control by southerners of federal trials meant sympathetic acquittal of offenders then, as it does now. And the Civil Rights Act of 1875, the one attempt by Congress to engage in a comprehensive attempt at making the southern Negro a first-class citizen, met destruction at the hands of a conservative post-Reconstruction Court intent upon preserving a traditional concept of federal-state relations — a concept which Congress, in any event, was probably not seriously interested in disturbing.[24]

The third constitutional barrier confronting the radicals' program — and the second one they failed to surmount — was that of civil liberties, which then as now posed grave obstacles to the execution of an extensive civil rights program.

The radicals did not treat southerners as a subjugated and inferior conquered population deprived of all constitutional rights. Instead, they imposed a period of limited and very restricted military probation — designed to inhibit outright acts of rebellion and to guarantee Negro political rights rather than to carry out any sweeping revolution in the fundamentals of race relations. And they also imposed a very partial political probationary period upon a very limited segment of the southern population — the deprival of political rights as set forth in the Third Section of the Fourteenth Amendment — and then, in 1872, removed virtually all that remained even of that disability in a sweeping amnesty act.

So lax was radical control of the South that white southerners were enabled to engage in large-scale sabotage even of the limited congressional program as incorporated in the Fourteenth and Fifteenth amendments, long before the troops

---

[24] Alfred H. Kelly, "The Congressional Controversy over School Segregation, 1867–1875," *American Historical Review*, LXIV (April, 1959), 537–63.

were withdrawn, as the *Globe* and *Congressional Record* make clear.[25] In short, the congressional civil rights program foundered not only on the rock of federalism but on the shoals of traditional orthodox civil liberties procedures as well — procedures which could have been swept away only by the resort to revolutionary legitimacy rather than those consonant with constitutional orthodoxy.

The radicals, in short, did not attack seriously the constitutional barriers posed either by federal-state relations or by the Bill of Rights. They devised a program which, in spite of much shouting, actually protected and reinstituted the main elements of both, imposing only a series of legal-constitutional guarantees for Negro political and legal rights which would inevitably be left to southern federal courts to implement. Constitutional conservatism of this kind doomed the nominal objectives of the radical program and the nominal professions of radical congressmen to failure. They were, in short, not revolutionary radicals at all. Instead, they were rather conservative constitutional legitimists, operating well within the Hamiltonian-Marshall tradition.

We can very well understand the radicals' constitutional conservatism and the dilemmas their own doctrines posed for them, for after a lapse of a hundred years we find ourselves attempting once more, very much in the spirit of 1865 and 1866, to implement a program which will guarantee Negro political and civil rights in the South without rupturing the basic framework of federal-state relations or the guarantees of the Bill of Rights. A reading of that interesting and tragic book, the *Report of the United States Commission on Civil Rights, 1963*,[26] ought to impress upon us how difficult a task that is —

---

[25] See, for example, the bargaining in Congress over the passage of the Amnesty Act of 1872, *Congressional Globe*, 42 Cong., 2 sess., 3730–36.

[26] *Report of the United States Commission on Civil Rights, 1963* (Washington, D.C., 1963). See especially the sections on "Techniques

if, indeed, it is not an impossible one within the time-frame that appears to be available to our country in the present crisis in race relations. The radicals of a hundred years ago rejected without serious debate the argument for revolutionary legitimacy as a substitute for constitutional legitimacy. I close my commentary with a question: Will the rising crescendo of racial unrest in the United States allow us much longer to operate within the confines of the constitutional bulwarks which made the racial program a century ago unsolvable? In our new "Trial of the Constitution," there is not much time left to us.

---

of Discrimination and Difficulties of Enforcement," pp. 22–26. The commission's observations have been rendered obsolete only in a very partial and modest sense by passage of the Civil Rights Act of 1964.

RECONSTRUCTION AND THE NEGRO

JOHN HOPE FRANKLIN
University of Chicago

For more than a generation, there has been an increasing disposition, on the part of historians, to take another look at the Negro's role during the Reconstruction era. Indeed, it was as far back as 1910 that William E. B. Du Bois took issue with the early students of the period who had concluded, almost casually, that the Negro was a dupe, used by sinister whites for their own selfish ends, and that Negroes themselves had contributed substantially to the failure of Reconstruction. With a view to reaching all or most of the serious students of the period, Du Bois published an article in the *American Historical Review* in which he said,

Granted . . . that the negroes were to some extent venal but to a much larger extent ignorant and deceived, the question is: did they show any signs of a disposition to learn better things? The theory of democratic governments is not that the will of the people is always right, but rather that normal human beings of average intelligence will, if given a chance, learn the right and best course by bitter experience. This is precisely what negro voters showed indubitable signs of doing. First, they strove for schools to abolish ignorance, and second, a large and growing number of them revolted against the carnival of extravagance and stealing that marred the beginning of Reconstruction, and joined with the best elements to institute reform. . . .[1]

There is reason to doubt that Du Bois reached any considerable number of historians of the Reconstruction or, if he did, that he had any appreciable effect on the manner in which they viewed the critical years following the Civil War. The view that Reconstruction was a "tragic era" in which honest government disappeared from the South while Carpetbaggers and Scalawags manipulated Negro voters and functionaries for their own benefit continued to hold sway. The rise of the Ku Klux Klan in the years following World War I was a vivid reminder that the hooded knights had "saved" the South once and now they would save the entire nation from the evil forces that were always ready to take advantage of a situation.

In this atmosphere of deepening despair among Negroes, a young Negro historian, Alrutheus A. Taylor, sought to repair some of the damage. In several monographs and articles on South Carolina, Virginia, and Tennessee, he made a valiant attempt to rehabilitate the Negro during Reconstruction. While the situation differed markedly from state to state, Taylor was convinced that, in general, Negroes had not fared well at the hands of the white historians of the Reconstruction. In his study of Virginia he said:

The Negroes of Virginia . . . cannot be charged with the mistakes in the reconstruction of the State. White men, the majority of whom were Virginians themselves, were the office-holders in Virginia during the reconstruction. The number of Negroes elected to office never became sufficient to determine any definite policy of the government except in a few cases of exercising a balance of power between militant factions. Those Negroes who attained

---

[1] W. E. B. Du Bois, "Reconstruction and Its Benefits," *American Historical Review*, XV (July, 1910), 798.

office, moreover, were generally persons of intelligence or common sense and they gave a good account of themselves.[2]

If Taylor's impact was limited, if not negligible, it was not only because of the rather pedestrian and ineffective style in which his sound scholarship was couched, but also because there was no disposition on the part of the professional and lay public to consider a revision of the point of view that had become firmly entrenched by the time Taylor was writing. Much more influential than Taylor's works was the popularization of the now-classic view of the Negro during Reconstruction by Claude Bowers, whose best-selling *Tragic Era: The Revolution After Lincoln* was published in 1929. After viewing the coalition developing between northern whites and Negroes, Bowers asserted, "Left to themselves, the negroes would have turned for leadership to the native whites, who understood them best. This was the danger. Imperative, then, that they should be taught to hate — and teachers of hate were plentiful."[3] Bowers then proceeded to embroider the theme that Negro rule was widespread, Negro suffrage tragic, and Negro perfidy rampant.

Du Bois, who had first challenged the established view, was no more willing to accept that view in later years than he had been in 1910. Therefore, in 1935 he brought out his *Black Reconstruction*, with the significant subtitle: *An Essay Toward a History of the Part Which Black Folk Played in the Attempt to Reconstruct Democracy in America, 1860–1880*. Despite the rather halfhearted and unsuccessful attempt by Du Bois to fit the Reconstruction era into a prefabricated mold of Marxist dialectics, he did succeed in convincing many of his

[2] Alrutheus Ambush Taylor, *The Negro in the Reconstruction of Virginia* (Washington, D.C., 1926), p. 285. See also his *The Negro in South Carolina During Reconstruction* (Washington, D.C., 1924) and *The Negro in Tennessee, 1865–1880* (Washington, D.C., 1941).

[3] Claude Bowers, *The Tragic Era: The Revolution After Lincoln* (New York, 1929), p. 199.

readers that the old view of the Negro's part in Reconstruction was shot through with inconsistencies, distortions, misrepresentations, and downright falsifications. Full of passion and bitterness that was the product of many years of what he regarded as his futile efforts in the civil rights movement, Du Bois' reading of the Reconstruction era challenged virtually every conclusion that had been reached by the earlier students of the period.

Du Bois was convinced that Negroes had been betrayed by the federal government and by many of the so-called reformers, and he argued this point throughout his lengthy work. He saw in Andrew Johnson unspeakable prejudice and in Ulysses S. Grant a tragic weakness combined with a lack of understanding of the presidency that bordered on irresponsibility. He saw in the murder and violence perpetrated by the Klan the supreme expression of barbarism and the tragic destruction of an incipient wholesome relationship between the black and white lower classes. Finally, he concludes: "The attempt to make black men American citizens was in a certain sense all a failure, but a splendid failure. It did not fail where it was expected to fail. It was Athanasius contra mundum, with back to the wall, outnumbered ten to one, with all the world against him. And only in his hands and heart the consciousness of a great and just cause; fighting the battle of all the oppressed and despised humanity of every race and color, against the massed hirelings of Religion, Science, Education, Law, and brute forces."[4]

This is neither the time nor the place to review the work of Du Bois. I have given some attention to it elsewhere.[5] It is enough to say that after the publication of *Black Reconstruction* it would never again be possible to look at the period without raising serious doubts about earlier views of the Ne-

---

[4] W. E. B. Du Bois, *Black Reconstruction* (New York, 1935), p. 708.
[5] See my review of the paperback edition in the New York *Herald Tribune*, July 5, 1964.

gro's role or without at least looking seriously at the bold positions taken by Du Bois. If Du Bois did nothing more — and he verily did much more — he made it possible for later reexaminations of the period to be viewed with greater tolerance and credibility. Thus, when Horace Mann Bond began in 1938 to revise the classic treatment of the Negro in Alabama Reconstruction that had been provided by Walter Lynwood Fleming, his work was widely regarded as a significant contribution to the history of the period. He provided convincing proof that neither the Negroes nor their allies were the heroes or villains of Alabama Reconstruction. The important ones to watch were a combination of native whites and northern businessmen who dominated the affairs of the state for the entire period.[6]

After 1940 the studies of the Negro in Reconstruction began to appear more frequently. In that year Samuel D. Smith brought out his study of the Negro in Congress.[7] A few years later Vernon L. Wharton published a penetrating study of the Negro in Mississippi. Within a few years C. Vann Woodward, Rayford W. Logan, George Bentley, Leslie Fishel, Otis Singletary, and Robert Durden published works bearing on various aspects of the Negro's role during Reconstruction. In more recent years the efforts have continued, and the recent work by LaWanda and John Cox, *Politics, Principle, and Prejudice*, and the volume by James McPherson in 1964, *The Struggle for Equality*, are outstanding in their handling of the role of the Negro in the political and social problems confronting the nation after the Civil War.[8]

[6] Horace Mann Bond, "Social and Economic Forces in Alabama Reconstruction," *Journal of Negro History*, XXIII (July, 1938), 290–348, and *Negro Education in Alabama: A Study in Cotton and Steel* (Washington, D.C., 1939).

[7] Samuel D. Smith, *The Negro in Congress, 1867–1901* (Chapel Hill, N.C., 1940).

[8] Vernon Lane Wharton, *The Negro in Mississippi, 1865–1890* (Chapel Hill, N.C., 1947); C. Vann Woodward, *The Strange Career*

It would, of course, be folly to suggest that we now have an adequate picture of the Negro during Reconstruction. We still know *all too little* about the relationship between Negroes, Carpetbaggers, and Scalawags. The picture of the Negro in Congress is far from complete. What kind of party men were they; were they race men or merely the representatives of their congressional districts? No one has yet given us a full account of the Negro in the early days of peace: what the role was of the Negro conventions in 1865 and 1866, how many actually were in a position to assume leadership roles, and what they wanted from the state and federal governments. We need to know a great deal more than we now know about Negro *officeholders* at the *state and local* levels and the reactions of Negroes to the growing indifference of the federal government to their needs and their plights as well as their aspirations. In other words, we have *just begun* to see the results of the extensive reexamination of the role of the Negro during Reconstruction, and it would not be too much to say that at least some of the recent works could themselves bear critical reexamination.

Despite the fact that the student of Reconstruction can hardly be satisfied with what is now known about the Negro's role, he already has sufficient knowledge to conclude that

---

of Jim Crow (New York, 1951); Rayford W. Logan, *The Negro in American Life and Thought* (New York, 1954); George R. Bentley, *A History of the Freedmen's Bureau* (Philadelphia, 1955); Leslie Fishel, "The Negro in Northern Politics, 1870–1900," *Mississippi Valley Historical Review*, XLII (December, 1955), 466–89; Otis Singletary, *Negro Militia and Reconstruction* (Austin, Tex., 1957); Robert F. Durden, *James Shepherd Pike: Republicanism and the American Negro, 1850–1882* (Durham, N.C., 1957); LaWanda and John H. Cox, *Politics, Principle, and Prejudice, 1865–1866* (New York, 1963); and James McPherson, *The Struggle for Equality: Abolitionists and the Negro in the Civil War and Reconstruction* (Princeton, N.J., 1964). See also Joel Williamson, *After Slavery* (Chapel Hill, N.C., 1965), and Kenneth M. Stampp, *The Era of Reconstruction, 1865–1877* (New York, 1965).

some modification of the old view is fully justified. It would be well, therefore, to take notice of some of the new ways of looking at the problem and to examine their implications for the study of the general problem of Reconstruction.

As historians have viewed the early weeks and months following the close of the Civil War, they have had a good deal to say about the desperate plight of the freedmen. It is, of course, difficult to exaggerate this situation, and there has been much emphasis on the freedman's lack of competence to care for himself in a condition of freedom. Indeed, there has been much emphasis on the freedman who, in consequence of his ignorance and inexperience, was the ready prey of any and all who might seek to exploit him. There was more than a semblance of truth in this as it applied to the vast majority of Negroes. This view does not, however, give sufficient consideration to the not inconsiderable number of Negroes who, by training and experience, were quite prepared in 1865 to take care of themselves and even to assume some leadership roles.

In 1860 there were some 488,000 free Negroes in the United States, of whom 261,000 — slightly more than one-half — lived in the slave states. Although the teaching of slaves and free Negroes to read and write was strictly forbidden by law in the slave states, thousands of slaves and free Negroes actually became literate. There were clandestine schools for Negroes in many communities in the South. In 1850, according to the census returns, there were 68 free Negroes attending school in Charleston, 53 in Mobile, 1,008 in New Orleans, and 1,453 in Baltimore.[9] In numerous instances slaveholders taught their human chattel to read and write. Laws forbidding the teaching of slaves were for people on the other plantations; masters

---

[9] A table containing this information, drawn from the Seventh Census, is in E. Franklin Frazier, *The Negro in the United States* (New York, 1957), p. 74.

did whatever they pleased regarding their own slaves. And if they saw fit, they taught their slaves to read and write. Frederick Douglass received his first instruction from his mistress. Isaiah T. Montgomery of Mississippi received sufficient training to become the confidential accountant for his master, the brother of Jefferson Davis.[10]

Meanwhile, Negroes were attending schools in many parts of the North. In 1850 there were more than 2,000 Negroes in Philadelphia; New York and Boston reported more than 1,400 each, while cities such as Providence, Brooklyn, New Haven, and Cincinnati each had several hundred Negroes in school.[11] In some communities, such as Boston after 1855, they attended desegregated schools, while in other communities segregated education was the rule. In any case, the number of literate Negroes was steadily increasing.

It might actually be possible to compile some rather impressive figures on Negro literacy, especially when one recalls that many Negroes were educated abroad and when one adds to this number those who began their education in schools established by religious and philanthropic agencies during the war years. The point, however, is not to emphasize the general increase in literacy among Negroes — important as that may be — but to underscore the fact that by the end of the Civil War thousands of Negroes in the North and South were able to read and write. A further point is that in their various organizations — religious and benevolent — Negroes had opportunities to use their education and acquire experience in the management of their affairs.

One of the best proofs we have of the level of literacy and education of a considerable group of Negroes by 1865 is in

----

[10] Carter G. Woodson, *The Education of the Negro Prior to 1860* (Washington, D.C., 1919), p. 315. I am indebted to Professor Horace M. Bond for his unpublished studies on the literacy of Negroes in the South at the end of the Civil War.

[11] Frazier, *op. cit.*, p. 74.

their organizational activities. Within the first year following the close of the war Negroes in the North and South met in conventions to consider their common problems. These are the months that many historians have described as months of wandering and drifting on the part of the freedmen. Many of them did drift — from place to place — to "test" their freedom. Others, however, did not drift. Instead, they met in convention at Alexandria, Norfolk, Raleigh, Savannah, Charleston, Vicksburg, Nashville, and Cleveland to give attention to the problems they faced. The deliberations were orderly and dignified, and they were carefully recorded.

It is not too much to say that some of the representations made by these all-Negro conventions in 1865 are eloquent, and they give evidence not only of ample training but of a degree of understanding of the function of government that must have surprised many observers. For example, in their letter to President Andrew Johnson in May, 1865, a group of North Carolina Negroes said:

Some of us are soldiers and have had the privilege of fighting for our country in this war. Since we have become Freemen, and been permitted the honor of being soldiers, we begin to feel that we are men, and are anxious to show our countrymen that we can and will fit ourselves for the creditable discharge of the duties of citizenship. We want the privilege of voting. It seems to us that men who are willing on the field of danger to carry the muskets of Republics in the days of peace ought to be permitted to carry its ballots; and certainly we cannot understand the justice of denying the elective franchise to men who have been fighting for the country, while it is freely given to men who have just returned from four years fighting against it.[12]

These are the words of literate people, perfectly capable of thinking through their problems and perfectly aware of their betrayal by their own government.

During these years, thanks to the increasing educational

---

[12] New York *Daily Tribune*, May 19, 1865.

opportunities provided by the Freedmen's Bureau and other agencies and thanks to their own organizational activities, many Negroes were rapidly assimilating the training and experience they needed to become participants in the affairs of their government. They therefore saw nothing unusual about their desire to enjoy the franchise, and more and more of them indicated such a desire. Inevitably many whites, especially those in the former Confederate states, raised questions about their qualifications and asserted that they lacked education and experience. Ths was the first time that such questions had been seriously raised since the ratification of the federal Constitution. Some Negroes thought these questions irrelevant, while others were certain that they could qualify if a reasonable test were fairly administered. Surely, all Negroes knew that race rather than education or experience was the major consideration in the suffrage question. All over the country there was some resistance to the enfranchisement of Negroes regardless of their educational qualifications, while in the South Negroes knew that they did not have the slightest chance of becoming enfranchised as long as the former Confederates were in power.

With no opportunity to participate in the political decisions regarding their own future, Negroes — even those who were college and university graduates — were unable to intervene effectively at any point. They were compelled, therefore, to accept decisions made for them by their former masters and the other whites who were eligible to serve their states under the Lincoln and Johnson plans of Reconstruction. Not only were Negroes without any voice in the decisions about their future, but they were also without any protection against the mistreatment or injustices to which they were subjected by the decision-makers. They *could and did* protest the enactment of harsh black codes by the state legislatures, but their protests were scarcely heard in the state capitals or even in Washington.

The absence of protection for the former slaves in the crucial first years following the end of the Civil War is one of the very remarkable phenomena of the early Reconstruction era. Even if one should argue — unsuccessfully, I believe — that the former masters continued to have the best interests of their former slaves in mind, there were the millions of whites, indeed the vast majority of southern whites, who had not been slaveholders. Many of them had much antipathy not only for the institution of slavery but for slaves as well. Whatever the attitude of former slaveholders or of nonslaveholders, the freedmen were left exposed to them and at their mercy. This was, of course, because of the rapid demobilization of the Union Army and the preoccupation of the military leaders with that process.

From the time that the Secretary of War issued the demobilization order on April 28, 1865, the troops were to be mustered out at the staggering rate of 300,000 per month. It was simply impossible to process that many men with the machinery in existence, but a vigorous effort was made to comply with the order. Within six months after the war's end more than 800,000 of the 1,034,064 officers and men in the United States Army had been demobilized. By the end of 1865 the government had 150,000 troops for all purposes, including garrisoning frontier posts and fighting the Indians, as well as supervising postwar operations in the South. Thus, by the end of December, 1865, North and South Carolina had 352 officers and 7,056 enlisted men. In the entire Division of the Gulf the number of white troops had been reduced to 10,000 men. There were vast stretches of territory in the former Confederacy where no Union soldier appeared after the late spring of 1865.[13]

By the close of the Civil War some 186,000 Negroes had

---

[13] House Executive Document, vol. 3, *Report of the Secretary of War for 1866*, 39 Cong., 2 sess. (Washington, D.C., 1867), p. 58.

seen service in the Army of the United States. They were not demobilized at quite the rate of white soldiers. They had no businesses and professions and jobs to which to return. There was no reason for them to make an immediate return to civilian life. If anyone could be spared from civilian life, it was the Negro serviceman. Some former Confederates would claim, of course, that the Negro troops were being detained for the specific purpose of humiliating the prostrate South. There is not a shred of evidence to support this claim. Surely most of the Negro troops themselves had no interest in committing acts of recrimination, and the official reports on their conduct support this view, local complaints to the contrary notwithstanding. One of the commanding officers in Arkansas said that his regiment of Negro soldiers was so preoccupied with learning to read and write that they had time for little else. Indeed, not all whites complained of Negro troops. To offset the complaints against Negro troops in southern Georgia, all the principal citizens of Jasper, Florida, petitioned for the return of a company of colored troops which had been ordered from there.[14] The point here is that in 1865 and 1866 there was not a sufficient number of United States troops, white or black, to provide even a semblance of protection for the 4,000,000 freedmen. The only protection they had was at the hands of the former Confederates, who hardly recognized any rights of Negroes that they were bound to respect.

When Congress took over the program of Reconstruction in 1867, the military supervision that had been reinstituted as the new governments were established was not only of short duration, but was, on the whole, ineffective. As soon as the new governments showed signs of stability the troops were withdrawn. In November, 1869, there were only 1,112 federal

---

[14] *Report of the Joint Committee on Reconstruction*, 39 Cong., 1 sess. (Washington, D.C., 1866), part 3, pp. 127, 44.

soldiers in Virginia, including those at Fortress Monroe. In Mississippi, at the same time, there were 716 officers and men scattered over the state.[15] Since state militias could not be established without the permission of the federal government, the Reconstruction governments — and the Negroes — were with little or no protection from the antigovernment Ku Klux Klan and other guerrillas that sprang up all over the South. The situation became so desperate that Congress finally gave permission in 1869 for North Carolina, South Carolina, Florida, Alabama, Louisiana, and Arkansas to organize state militias. Some of the other states proceeded to organize militias without congressional authorization.

It was not always easy to enlist a sufficient number of white men to fill the militia quotas, and under the new dispensation Negroes were eligible anyway. To many white observers, the number of Negro militiamen seemed excessive, and the inference was drawn, as it was drawn in 1865, that the presence of such large numbers of armed Negroes was for the purpose of humiliating the whites. Because of the growing hostility to these armed groups and because of the increasing strength of the enemies of the Reconstruction governments, the state militias contributed, in a sense, to the downfall of the governments they were supposed to protect.[16] It cannot be argued, however, that armed men, whether white or black, or whether federal or state, were of such numbers as to constitute a military occupation of the South. And without such occupation, the Negroes of the former Confederate states became the special targets and the victims of the groups who were determined to overthrow congressional Reconstruction.

Viewed in this light, Negroes became the easy prey of the hooded Klansmen and others of their ilk. The federal troops,

---

[15] John Hope Franklin, *Reconstruction After the Civil War* (Chicago, 1961), p. 120.

[16] Otis Singletary, *op. cit.*, p. 152.

if they were present at all, were insufficient in numbers to have any significant effect. President Grant, moreover, was most reluctant to dispatch troops to troubled areas and did so only when the situation became bloody and desperate. The state militias, with their large Negro contingents, merely fired the antagonism of those opposed to the Reconstruction governments and set them off on a reign of bloody terror that was unworthy of a civilized community. In the congressional hearings on the Klan terror in 1871, one Negro woman who occupied land that the whites wanted gave this testimony:

They whipped me from the crown of my head to the soles of my feet. I was just raw. The blood oozed out through my frock all around the waist, clean through. . . . After I got away from them that night I ran to my house. My house was torn down. I went in and felt where my bed was . . . I went to the other corner of the house and felt for my little children and I could not see them. . . . Their father lay out to the middle of the night, and my children lay out there too.[17]

The period of congressional Reconstruction has been described by some as Negro rule, and the new governments in the South have been described as Black and Tan governments. The clear implication is that Negroes dominated the governments of the former Confederacy or that at least their role and their vote were crucial. Today, few, if any, serious students of the period would countenance any such description. It should be added, somewhat hastily, however, that many politicians and laymen who today attack civil rights and voting legislation do so on the ground that it would deliver the South to the Negro, whose role would be reminiscent of the Reconstruction era. While such a claim is both specious and fallacious, there persists the view, even among some serious

---

[17] *Testimony Taken by the Joint Committee to Inquire into the Condition of Affairs in the Late Insurrectionary States* (Washington, D.C., 1872), XIII, 59 ff. They said that they would not be satisfied until she left the land.

students, that the Negro's influence during congressional Reconstruction was considerable and even decisive.

The only states in which Negroes were in the government in any considerable number were South Carolina, Mississippi, and Louisiana. In the first South Carolina legislature Negroes outnumbered whites eighty-seven to forty, but they controlled at no time any other branch of the state government. In Louisiana, they numbered forty-two out of eighty-four members of the lower house, although it should be remarked that the number is not precisely known because of the racial admixture of so many of the members. In Mississippi there were forty Negroes out of a total of 115 members in the first Reconstruction legislature. It is not necessary to review here the racial composition of the legislatures of the several states or of the other branches of the governments.[18] One can state categorically that Negroes did not rule anywhere in the South.

This is not to say that there were not any individual Negroes who were without responsibility and influence. Here one must recall that much of the Negro leadership was both literate and experienced. In the several southern states not only were there Negroes who emerged as leaders but also the black Carpetbaggers, so-called, who returned to their southern homes after many years of absence. Some who moved South had never lived there before. In South Carolina Francis L. Cardozo, who became secretary of state and later the state treasurer, was educated at the University of Glasgow and at London, while J. J. Wright, who became a member of the state supreme court, had been educated at the University of Pennsylvania and was a member of the Pennsylvania bar. In Alabama James T. Rapier, who became a member of Congress, had been sent to Canada by his white father to be educated. Jonathan Gibbs, who became secretary of state in Florida,

---

[18] See my *Reconstruction After the Civil War* for a more extensive discussion of this problem.

was a graduate of Dartmouth and had been a Presbyterian minister for several years before the beginning of the Civil War.

Obviously, these were exceptional men. After all, it would be unusual to find among the white members of these governments graduates of Glasgow, London, or Harvard. Most of the white *and* Negro leaders were self-made men, who, through perseverance, native ability, and sometimes a little bit of luck, made their way up to positions of influence and importance. Obviously also, there were some men in both races who made their way to power through chicanery, duplicity, and fraud. Once in power they used their positions, as one might expect, to advance their own interests, frequently at the expense of the welfare of the larger community.

One principal reason why there was not and could not have been any such thing as Negro rule is not merely because the Negroes had insufficient political power but also because the coalition to which they belonged was both loose and ineffective. One group in the so-called coalition, the Scalawags, belonged to it not because they shared the Negro's ideals or aspirations but because they were qualified under the strict requirements laid down by the Congress. The other group, the Carpetbaggers, contained people whose views differed from each other almost as much as their general view differed from the former Confederates. Some were investors who were politically neutral, some were Union soldiers who just liked the South, some were clever politicians, some were teachers in Negro schools, and indeed some were Negroes. It is inconceivable that these many groups could have agreed on a political or social program, and in the absence of substantial agreement the Negro wielded little influence and received few benefits.[19]

---

[19] Stanley Coben, "Northeastern Business and Radical Reconstruction: A Re-examination," *Mississippi Valley Historical Review*, XLVI (June, 1959), 67–90.

In the constitutional conventions and in the subsequent governments in each of the states, the groups making up the coalition were at odds with each other over such fundamental questions as the nature and amount of power to be vested in the state government, the matter of public education, and what, if anything, should be done to guarantee the rights of Negroes. Many of the native whites went over to the opposition when it appeared that the governments were moving toward equal rights for Negroes. Many northerners became lukewarm when the new governments threatened to impose restrictions on capital investments. Others from the North, the idealists, became disgusted with the manner in which the governments came under the influence of the venal business interests of all groups. Small wonder, under the circumstances, that they were unable to agree on the outlines of programs of welfare, social reform, and public education — conveniently segregated almost everywhere.

The Reconstruction governments in the South have been described by almost all historians as radical. While the description is almost permanently fixed, it does not appear to be very accurate. If some of the governments were corrupt and extravagant — and not all of them were — they were very much like state governments in other parts of the country at the time; indeed the federal government was not without its crooks and knaves. If some of them pressed for welfare legislation and public education, they were seeking to close the gap that had separated them for a generation from the progressive states of the Northeast. If they moved toward universal suffrage, they were following the lead of states in the North and some countries abroad. The only possible radical aspect was that, at the insistence of the federal government, Negroes had to be included in the new concept of universal education. But when one considers the growing number of Negroes who were acquiring education and experience, many of them could meet the standards that had not been required or expected of any other group in the history of American suffrage.

There is something quite tragic about the picture of the Negro as he entered upon his first century of freedom. In the beginning he was denied equal rights as a citizen on the ground that he was not qualified, and there was a disposition to deny him the opportunity to become qualified on the ground that he was unfit for citizenship and equality. But there is also something quite tragic about the picture of the United States as it entered its second century of independence. In the beginning it had captured the imagination of peoples around the world with its ringing declaration that all men were created equal. By the time that it had reached the respectable if not venerable age of one hundred years, it was reconsidering its earlier declaration, and neither the Fourteenth nor the Fifteenth amendments were sufficient to extend equal rights to all its citizens. It was the Negro, released from 250 years of human bondage, who brought about this reconsideration; but it was also the Negro who challenged, even dared, the country to deny its earlier pronouncements. If Reconstruction did nothing else, it called attention to the inescapable fact that the United States would have to move forward on the basis of equality, even if it included the Negro, or it would be compelled to retrogress to a point where its distinctiveness would no longer be valid. This has been the torment of the last hundred years, and it began with the Negro during Reconstruction.

Comment on
John Hope Franklin's Paper

AUGUST MEIER
Roosevelt University

Mr. Franklin's paper is an excellent statement of what we now know about Negroes and their role during the Reconstruction period. Because he has so thoroughly cleared the way, I would like to devote the time allotted me to indicate some of the areas in Negro Reconstruction history which I think would be fruitful topics for further research. Or, to phrase it differently, I will indicate some of the directions in which "the extensive reexamination of the role of the Negro during Reconstruction," to which Mr. Franklin refers, may be likely to take us.

I am particularly pleased that Mr. Franklin called our attention to the somewhat neglected works of A. A. Taylor. At the time they appeared, about forty years ago, his volumes on South Carolina and Virginia were extraordinary studies. His books served as the model for Wharton's later volume on Mississippi, and also for the more recent books on the Negro in the Carolinas in the years after Reconstruction. And I suspect that his volume on South Carolina was of more than incidental value to Simkins and Woody in the preparation of their work on Reconstruction in that state — a book which, though not entirely satisfactory in its treatment of Negroes, probably was more influential than W. E. B. Du Bois' *Black Reconstruction* in bringing the general run of white historians to begin a reconsideration of their views on the period.[1] We are greatly in need of comparable studies on other states, particularly Alabama, Georgia, and Louisiana.[2] Moreover, the resourceful and imaginative scholar, willing to dig into local history, could make a real contribution by making a careful study of a plantation area like the Black Belt counties surrounding Selma, Alabama — itself a veritable museum.

We also need a number of specialized studies, cutting across state lines, especially in economic and social history. In general I think we can look at the following topics in two distinct but interrelated ways — first from the point of view of the history of the Negro community considered by itself, and second by trying to answer the question, "How did Negroes *function* in Reconstruction history?"

First of all, I think we must ask ourselves the question, "How did Negroes view Reconstruction?" Of course there is no such abstraction as "The Negro"; at the very least we have

---

[1] Alrutheus Ambush Taylor, *The Negro in the Reconstruction of Virginia* (Washington, D.C., 1926) and *The Negro in South Carolina During Reconstruction* (Washington, D.C., 1924); Vernon Lane Wharton, *The Negro in Mississippi, 1865–1890* (Chapel Hill, N.C., 1947); George B. Tindall, *South Carolina Negroes, 1877–1900* (Columbia, S.C., 1952); Frenise Logan, *The Negro in North Carolina, 1876–1894* (Chapel Hill, N.C., 1964); Francis B. Simkins and Robert H. Woody, *South Carolina During Reconstruction* (Chapel Hill, N.C., 1932).

[2] Since this paper was written, two significant state studies have appeared: Joel R. Williamson, *After Slavery: The Negro in South Carolina During Reconstruction, 1861–1877* (Chapel Hill, N.C., 1965), and Joe M. Richardson, *The Negro in the Reconstruction of Florida* (Tallahassee, Fla., 1965).

to talk of northern Negroes and southern Negroes and of the Negro masses and the Negro elite. Even within these categories we will find variations. We have library shelves full of what whites were thinking on Reconstruction and its problems, but practically no consideration has been given to Negro thought and ideology during the period. For example, no one has investigated the Negro convention movement during the Civil War and afterwards. Although one recent study[3] has made a beginning in treating Negro thinking on the subject, much remains to be done. In this connection we ought to have a probing investigation of the degree to which Negroes influenced the thinking of white abolitionists and congressional radicals on such matters as civil rights and Negro suffrage. Perhaps, as was said during the discussion this afternoon, Negroes were not influential in affecting the policies of the white decision-makers, but the matter in any case needs careful study, for if indeed Negroes were of virtually no influence, this fact in itself tells us a good deal about the nature of American society at the time.

Elsewhere[4] I have suggested that in the South the elite Negroes and the masses assigned different priorities to their chief objectives. The masses, I said, wanted land of their own more than anything else, next they desired education, and they were concerned with civil and political rights to a somewhat lesser extent. Elite Negroes, on the other hand, seemed mainly concerned with obtaining political and civil rights, while for them settlement of the land question was a less weighty matter. I think that this whole thesis should be subjected to a searching investigation. We also need to pay more attention to the early events in the "strange career of Jim

---

[3] James M. McPherson, *The Struggle for Equality: Abolitionists and the Negro in the Civil War and Reconstruction* (Princeton, N.J., 1964).

[4] August Meier, *Negro Thought in America, 1880–1915* (Ann Arbor, Mich., 1963), Chap. I, "The Heritage of Reconstruction."

Crow," and to Negro protests against segregation. Negro protests against the star streetcars in New Orleans and the ride-ins in Louisville are fairly well known, but we need to know about the prevalence and character of such protests elsewhere. Then there were those Negroes who, discouraged with conditions in the United States, turned to emigration. Here and there we have references in the monographic literature to colonization activities, but a systematic study is lacking.

Then there is the vexatious matter of the freedmen's economic history. Here a host of questions comes to mind. Some years ago Roger Shugg described what happened to the plantation system in Louisiana,[5] but to what extent did the system survive in other states? To what extent did the ante-bellum landed aristocracy hold on to its land? To what extent was it replaced by northerners and by upward mobile southerners? The same questions apply, of course, to the handful of Negroes who were plantation owners.

Just how did the sharecropping system develop? Here and there in the monographic literature and from occasional articles, we can glean some suggestions, but we actually know very little about the matter. Was the pattern of the development of tenant farming the same in all parts of the South? What people were responsible for its growth? How important in encouraging the system was the lack of fluid capital? Did planters institute sharecropping in order to exploit the labor of the ex-slave, or did they resort to it because the freedmen were reluctant to sign contracts as laborers? Did the Negroes consider sharecropping a step forward on the road of upward economic mobility or a device to keep them down? Did the Freedmen's Bureau foster sharecropping because its officials thought the system would uplift and protect the Negro and because, in effect, they had to find a way of getting around

---

[5] Roger W. Shugg, *Origins of Class Struggle in Louisiana* (Baton Rouge, 1939), Chap. VIII.

the white planters' refusal to pay decent wages? Or did the bureau's personnel encourage sharecropping arrangements because of a paternalistic and prejudiced attitude toward Negroes and because they interpreted the Negroes' refusal to work at the terms set by the planters as evidence of laziness rather than as justifiable dissatisfaction with the wages offered? Or were the bureau's representatives forced into sharecropping agreements by virtue of the intransigent attitude of the planters? If, as is likely, several factors were involved, how did they interact to produce the sharecropping system?

The whole matter of Negro migration during Reconstruction should be reexamined. The evidence suggests that Negroes aimed to be cash-renters and farmowners. It is likely that Negro migration stemmed from this desire for economic advancement. The extent of Negro migration has been grossly exaggerated by historians with a white southern bias, but in the half century after the Civil War there was a general southwestward movement of the center of Negro population and a tendency for the racial proportions in the population of certain counties to change drastically. The roots of these trends during Reconstruction should be analyzed.

The Negro urban artisan and entrepreneur has not been given serious attention outside of the monographs on the Reconstruction Negro in a handful of specific states. In a number of towns free Negroes dominated certain skilled trades at the end of the slave era, and Negroes were still prominent in these into the twentieth century. But their situation gradually eroded. At the same time, the market for Negro entrepreneurs shifted from white customers to Negroes. What factors caused this decline? To what extent was it a continuation of antebellum trends? To what extent did this decline of the Negro artisan-entrepreneur with white customers occur during Reconstruction? Can one discern varying patterns in different types of cities?

We have referred to the role of the Freedmen's Bureau in

shaping the economic status of the ex-slaves. At least as important, and in the long run clearly a more constructive contribution, was its work in education. The bias of even the most recent book on the Freedmen's Bureau [6] is so patent that a careful reevaluation of the bureau's work is a necessity. This reevaluation should focus more on the Negroes and less on the white missionaries, generals, and politicians.

If research on the Freedmen's Bureau has largely fallen into the hands of what I refer to as the "cynical" school of historians, the same is also true of the two leading volumes on the northern missionaries in the South.[7] Except for an unsatisfactory treatment of the work of the northern Methodists, the whole story of the religious and educational work of the northern denominations, white and black, among southern Negroes remains practically a virgin field. The story of Negro education is, of course, closely intertwined with the work of the northern churches. Actually, except for a study of Negro colleges in Georgia and an excellent unpublished dissertation on the history of the American Missionary Association,[8] we appear to be without a serious scholarly study of the development of Negro education in the South.

The history of the development of the Negro churches during Reconstruction — especially of the Baptists and the three Methodist connections — is particularly important because of the vital role they played in the Negro community. Along with the mutual benefit societies and fraternal orders — which were themselves often quasi-religious in their ritual and orientation

---

[6] George R. Bentley, *A History of the Freedmen's Bureau* (Philadelphia, 1955).

[7] Henry L. Swint, *The Northern Teacher in the South, 1862–1870* (Nashville, 1941); Ralph Morrow, *Northern Methodism and Reconstruction* (East Lansing, Mich., 1956).

[8] Willard Range, *The Rise and Progress of Negro Colleges in Georgia* (Athens, Ga., 1951); Richard B. Drake, "The American Missionary Association and the Southern Negro, 1861–1888" (unpublished Ph.D. dissertation, Emory University, 1957).

— the churches served as the arena for the fulfillment of leadership aspirations. This situation arose out of the fact that ordinarily Negroes were denied participation in the civic and political life of their communities. Many of the Reconstruction political leaders were, in fact, ministers; some of the leading ones among them were northern ministers who found in the South opportunities not open to them in the North.

Any study of the Negro community and its structure must thus begin with the church and the mutual benefit society and with the leaders which these institutions produced. In addition, the study of the Negro community during Reconstruction should examine the development and role of the other elite groups, especially the artisans and the businessmen, the nature of the Negro class structure, and the degree of economic and social mobility that existed. I think varying patterns will emerge in different areas. In addition to rural-urban differences, there were probably differences among various cities. Thus preliminary research which I have done on the history of the Negro upper class in Charleston, New Orleans, Durham, and Atlanta suggests that in the old coastal cities, which had substantial free Negro populations, the upper class was formed of members of the old free-Negro group. On the other hand in the newer Piedmont cities, the upper class consisted chiefly of former house slaves and former slave artisans, who had been owned by prosperous whites. Occupationally, however, both groups tended to be similar. That is, along with a few professional men, they were artisans and businessmen with white customers. The evidence I have also suggests that the Negro elite became closely tied to the missionary schools, in particular those of the American Missionary Association. It was to these schools that the elite, who were often without much formal education themselves, sent their children. To these schools ambitious youth of humble origins also gravitated. Thus the Congregationalist schools like Avery Institute in Charleston, Fisk and Atlanta universities in Nashville and

Atlanta, and Straight College in New Orleans functioned both as transmitters of northern polite culture to upper-class youth, and as a route of upward mobility for people of middle and lower social status.

Closely related to the subject of Negro class structure is that of Negro leadership. In his book, *Reconstruction After the Civil War*,[9] Mr. Franklin observes that the top Negro political leaders tended to be ministers and teachers, and that they generally possessed a relatively high degree of education. If possible it would be good to have careful statistical studies of the secondary ranks of Negro leaders. Other questions come to mind in this connection: How many Negro leaders were "carpet-baggers"? Was the northern-born group better educated than the southern-born leaders? How many of the latter had been born free? Of those who were ex-slaves, how many had been house servants and skilled artisans? Were there any former slave drivers among them? To what extent did the ante-bellum elite of free people move into leadership positions? Did ante-bellum Negro slaveowners play any leadership role during Reconstruction? What were the routes by which the leaders achieved their position? Why, for example, were the political leaders disproportionately ministers and teachers? Why were so few businessmen? Is there any connection between the occupational origins of Negro politicians and the fact that the ante-bellum Negro artisans had been closely connected with the white elite by kinship and economic ties?

Today, even the textbooks are generally coming around to note the fact that Negroes served in major political offices during Reconstruction, and that these officials were less corrupt than their white counterparts. And no scholarly work or book of readings discussing the abolitionists is now complete without at least some references to, and quotations from, such

---

[9] John Hope Franklin, *Reconstruction After the Civil War* (Chicago, 1961).

men as Frederick Douglass, John Mercer Langston, and William Still. In recent years there have appeared certain very fine works, breaking important new ground, dealing with Reconstruction politics and the abolitionists.[10] Yet scholars still fail to give us any clear idea as to how the Negro leaders and abolitionists actually functioned within the Republican party or the antislavery movement. These volumes leave the impression that on most matters it was the whites, not the Negroes, who were the decision-makers. I must say that anyone who has been a close observer of today's civil rights movement, in which Negroes are the leaders and whites are the followers and foot-soldiers, receives a curious sensation from reading these volumes. It is as if the Negro leaders in the past served largely as symbols, rather than as actors. Whether this impression is due to the prejudice of the white radicals and abolitionists, who declared their belief in racial equality but acted with paternalism and condescension, or whether — as in the case of Samuel Denny Smith's volume of some years ago on the Negro in Congress [11] — it is due to the bias of historians, is not entirely clear. Perhaps it is due to both.

Today, a hundred years after Reconstruction, the South and the nation are again being compelled to face the challenge of the gap between our moral values and the facts of racial discrimination. For the second time the American people are

---

[10] Eric L. McKitrick, *Andrew Johnson and Reconstruction* (Chicago, 1960); LaWanda and John H. Cox, *Politics, Principle, and Prejudice, 1865–1866* (New York, 1963); McPherson, *The Struggle for Equality*. Kenneth Stampp's *The Era of Reconstruction, 1865–1877* (New York, 1965), which appeared after this paper was given, is a recent synthesis utilizing the conclusions of these scholars. McPherson, who gives more attention to Negro thinking and activity than most scholars, tends to accept the protestation of the white abolitionists as to their belief in racial equality, although the evidence in his own book indicates that they tended to treat the Negroes paternalistically, to do things for them rather than with them.

[11] Samuel Denny Smith, *The Negro in Congress, 1870–1901* (Chapel Hill, N.C., 1940).

undergoing a crisis of conscience on the race question. It is understandable, therefore, that historians are looking at Reconstruction with new eyes. But somehow the American white man still seems more preoccupied with his own guilt, with his own handling of the racial situation, than with how Negroes felt and acted. As it is with the general public, so it seems to be with historians.

We are now beginning to get a handful of extraordinary works, describing with probing realism how northern whites behaved during Reconstruction. But to a large extent what we are getting is not the history of Negroes, but the history of what whites were thinking and doing about Negroes. This situation is not, of course, limited to Reconstruction historians. The historiography of the ante-bellum abolitionist movement in recent years is, if anything, more seriously deficient. One exception to this generalization, however, should be mentioned. I refer to Mrs. Rose's brilliant and perceptive volume on the South Carolina sea islands which deals incisively and sympathetically with the ambivalences of the white missionaries and abolitionists on the one hand, and with the feelings and actions of the Negro freedmen on the other.[12]

What we must do therefore is to break out of the mold of treating Negro history chiefly as the history of what whites do about or to Negroes. We have to focus far more upon the actions of Negroes themselves. Basically, we must ask new questions. We must ask how Negroes actually functioned in the social context of Reconstruction. And we must do so with the realization that even the groups that championed the Negro's rights were not completely egalitarian in their actions. In short we must do our research, keeping in mind that Negroes were not chiefly bystanders to events in which whites were the actors, but were also people who were themselves active participants in our history.

---

[12] Willie Lee Rose, *Rehearsal for Reconstruction: The Port Royal Experiment* (Indianapolis, 1964).

SOUTH AMERICA LOOKS AT NORTH AMERICAN RECONSTRUCTION

HARRY BERNSTEIN
Brooklyn College,
City University of New York

The last one hundred years, not the first, are the hardest. This centennial will be a reminder for Latin America of its coexistence with a far more prosperous and democratic United States, within the same hemisphere. The hare and the tortoise are the obvious analogy: the United States forged ahead after its Reconstruction; South America did not.

South America also faced Reconstruction and restoration in 1865 and 1870. Bruised and split by civil wars, few Latin Americans had energy to look northward for any inspiration or example. Political civil war and international wars were bad enough. Internal crusades against each other in the name of religion made their civil wars very intense. On the other hand, they were spared the bitter feeling of white against black. Slavery was not their issue. Except in Brazil and Cuba it had been abolished in most of Latin America long before.

Latin American Reconstruction did not take the form of an army of occupation holding a part of a country. Military victory and law enforcement did not go that far. Any comparison between North and South American Reconstruction stops here. Moreover, political assassination was not the curtain-raiser to Reconstruction. Contrary to impressions, major Latin American leaders have never been assassinated. Juárez, Bolívar, San Martín, and many others were sent to exile. They were not marked for murder.

Lincoln's assassination left a shock. The loss brought a deep and sad sense of personal and spiritual leaderlessness, even in South America. So deep and widespread was the sentiment, that even at the risk of provocation, it is worth suggesting that April, 1865, may well date the rise of anti-yanquí feeling and antimaterialism among Latin America's intellectual and student idealists. It certainly never existed before.

For many Latin Americans this was the painful note. North American Reconstruction opened with that sound. The death of Lincoln overshadowed the abolition of slavery and was far more discussed. In fact, Lincoln was identified with the end of the ugly picture of slavery. He killed the monster. But Reconstruction, on the other hand, killed off only the rural democracy which so many Latin American travelers admired. The charm of landscape and small-town life came to an end after Reconstruction; big business and corporations replaced these pleasant sights. Latin Americans had critical things to say about vulgarity, the new rich, and the new figures of the day. There are exceptions, to be sure. The Mexican Matías Romero, who did not like or trust Lincoln, took a realistic view of both the assassination and the Reconstruction. He preferred to see that the Republican party of Reconstruction days was the right North American group for Mexico "to play ball with."

The thirty years between Reconstruction and the Spanish American War gave enough time for all these feelings to take hold. The generation gave way to the idealism of students and intellectuals. The anti-yanquí and anti–Wall Street slogans of 1900 began to appear. The United States acquired a "new look."

However, Latin America has never been that intellectual. South America had other troubles in 1870: the enormous masses of illiterates kept their heads down. They probably did not even know of North America. As far as the masses of people went, the Indians, mestizos, mulattoes, Negroes, and immigrants had no noticeable awareness of North America. True, the North American missionary had brought Christianity down to many of them, but most people were outside the bounds of Inter-American outlook. Then as now, even a hundred years later, the South American Negro knew next to nothing about the North American Negro; neither had made any effort after Reconstruction to get in touch with the other. Nor has there ever been any people-to-people contact between the Indians. None of this should be surprising. Except for the Emancipation Act, one or two speeches of Wendell Phillips, and the Brazilian translations of *Uncle Tom's Cabin*, there is little evidence to show that the two great abolitionists of Brazil and the United States ever had much to do with each other. Only a few scholarly intellectuals, learned and scientific societies, and the governments had any direct, Inter-American contact with each other. The South American educated and middle classes preferred to look to Europe for their ideas, roots, and intellectual prejudices.

Neither the Reconstruction nor any other critical historical era has ever really shifted the basically European horizon of Latin America. Before and after the Reconstruction, it is true, the cultural axis of the New World increased, but without offsetting the European pull on Latin America. America and Europe were part of each other: cultural ancestry and constant environment. The New World and Old World need to be added together, not subtracted one from the other. That is what has made both South America and North America so Western, in addition to lying in the same hemisphere. It is as

great and harmful a fallacy to look upon Latin America as
non-Western as it is to look at North America that way. What
South America looked for in North America was their common Western tradition, differently used. This common heritage influenced the South American view of North American
Reconstruction, slavery, emancipation, and the restoration of
national-federal government.

Not many were able to notice this in 1865. Only the few
who traveled or lived in North America saw the Reconstruction close-up. They liked or disliked what they saw, but they
did not change opinion back home. Some did not want to.
When the cannon fire of the Latin American civil wars ended
by 1870, the view from their side of the bridge was perhaps
murky with disappointment, pessimism, and gunsmoke.

It is not easy to record the whole range of thoughts and feelings with which any individual compared his *patria* with the
post-Reconstruction United States. The answers depend on
people and places. How did the Latin American reality of
1870 jolt or please the sons of the founding fathers of 1810?
Some felt envy and jealous admiration of the United States.
Perhaps this feeling is basic throughout the hundred years of
this Reconstruction and centennial era. Some deplored boor-
ishness, money, vulgarity in the United States. Others saw in
its liberties, special institutions, and way of life a strength
which not only would carry through any Reconstruction
trouble, but would also leave enough over for Latin America
to emulate. Others looked for and saw neither a way of life
nor the ashes of slave institutions, but the triumph of strong,
centralized government and Union. The image of North
America, like beauty, is much in the eye of the beholder.
These were the images in the mind's eye of the Latin American observers.

A surprising number of Latin Americans traveled and lived
in the United States before and during Reconstruction. Three
or four are well known for what they said in their books: Sal-

vador Camacho Roldán of Colombia, Domingo F. Sarmiento of Argentina, and Matías Romero of Mexico. They are not only well known; they were all extremely intelligent in their separate interests. Camacho Roldán is a forerunner of modern sociology; Sarmiento, of public education; Romero, of Inter-American relations. Other Latin Americans who came up here in Reconstruction times are not so well known: Quintino Bocaiuva, the Brazilian republican, and André Rebouças, the Brazilian Negro.

On the general picture of "The United States in the Spanish American Mind," Dr. John T. Reid has recently put down in typescript the views of better-known travelers. He has given the cultural side of the post-Reconstruction in an investigation for the USIS. In my own *Making an Inter-American Mind* (Gainesville, Fla., 1961), a reverse view revealed what North American scientists, historians, and scholars had been learning about Latin American history and culture. The fact is, in both studies, that the image seen of Latin America, as well as the North American image, was caught only by a few. Both the masses of North America and the masses of South America had other things on their minds.

The Reconstruction era forms part of the large intellectual and cross-cultural history of the United States and Latin America. Travelers and Latin American intellectuals in this country nurtured these cultural relations. There was a great deal of serious effort to know about each other, even within the small numbers of those who were part of the process. This may not be the place to argue the Bolton Thesis of a common history of the Americas, but it is relevant to say here that the Reconstruction era at least stimulated a common historiography for the Americas.

The idea of a Greater American history even took book form by 1870.

The real Reconstruction, however, was not in the realm of ideas. The rebuilding of conditions and the passage of laws took priority. This is also what Latin Americans saw and evaluated. Some of them, especially Brazilians, saw slavery and agriculture as the essence of Reconstruction. But the same observer could combine cultural and scientific vision with a liberal concern for slavery. Such a person was José Carlos Rodrigues.

José Carlos Rodrigues was a famous Brazilian journalist, intellectual, bibliographer, and Protestant. He published the celebrated newspaper, *O Novo Mundo*, in New York City from 1870 to 1873. By this time, Louis Agassiz and William James had returned from Brazil, and Brazilian slavery was more publicized in the United States. Rodrigues thus knew and compared both systems and the effectiveness of abolition on both. He thought that the North American system of emancipation would be best for Brazil. So did many others of that day, who turned out to be wrong.

Rodrigues' views of slavery, the effectiveness of the Freedmen's Bureau, and military Reconstruction were probably the chief channels of information available to the Brazilians from the outside. He was highly esteemed, and his *O Novo Mundo* was very popular in Brazil. He also actively encouraged and financed Brazil–United States cultural relations. He supported the work of Charles Hartt in Brazil and the scholarships for the Brazilian students who came up to Cornell early in 1870.

The comparative slavery of Brazil and the United States was very much influenced by the shadow and image of Lincoln. His friends were everywhere in Latin America. He was the Great Emancipator who would also set the example for Brazil and Cuba. Even Rodrigues accepted that, although he also saw that emancipation in Brazil would have to obey Luso-Brazilian history.

There is no doubt that Brazil looked to emancipation in the United States for the idea, example, and inspiration. It left a mark. Emancipation, and Reconstruction later, meant for the

slaveowners a fear of the North American action being repeated in Brazil. But for those who were not slaveowners,
quite another point of view appeared. An idealistic enthus-
iasm arose among Brazilian abolitionists, liberals, and early
Republicans that the freeing of labor would build up an
artisan-based society. Even those who defended the more
"humane" treatment of the Brazilian slaves and a "kindlier"
image of the Brazilian slaveowner went on to borrow an antislavery spirit. A most important friend of the United States in
Brazil, A. C. Tavares Bastos, the famous liberal, drew his
readers' attention to the nature of comparative slavery in
North and South America. He opposed slavery in Brazil at the
same time that he defended the spirit of slavery there: "Certainly, our slave owners deserve some praises for the most part,
compared to the cynical cruelty of slave breeders in Dela-
ware, Maryland, Kentucky and Missouri, or to the savage ex-
cesses of some of the inhabitants of southern United States.
We have no deeds here like the lamentable picture of B.
Stowe, the slave hunt, the *lynch-law*, the legal prohibition of
all instruction and religious education. . . ."

But Tavares Bastos was down there and José Carlos Rodrigues was in North America, and Rodrigues saw slavery in the
United States somewhat differently. His views on Brazilian
slavery and the North American Reconstruction are not part
of any historian's polemic, but are worth noticing just the
same.

He did not believe that United States slavery was bad or
that Brazilian slavery was good. He did not share the current
view of his compatriot, A. C. Tavares Bastos. He insisted that
southern slavery, unlike Brazilian, had given the North
American Negro a real Christian and moral sense of worth,
honor, and conduct. He also maintained that slavery itself
before the Civil War, and the Freedmen's Bureau since Reconstruction, had made a skilled worker and a dedicated farmer of the former slave. He sorely deplored the absence of this

in Brazil. He did not go into any comparison of Catholic and Protestant values affecting slave and citizen.

Many other Brazilian progressives were convinced that the Reconstruction in the United States would create a free Negro farmer out of the slave and bring a skilled labor force into society. The climate for this Brazilian belief was not only favored by the North American example, both Brazil and North America, perhaps, were influenced by the logic of the noted French geographer, Elisée Reclus. In that era of French interventionism in Mexico, Reclus had been traveling in Colombia and the coastal Caribbean. This Frenchman, writing upon the Negro in this hemisphere, preceded by a century the better-known Swede Gunnar Myrdal, who wrote only of the Negro in the United States.

Brazilians leaned a great deal upon Reclus' article in the *Revue de Deux Mondes* (March-April, 1863). There, he had drawn up a sort of prophecy of the North American Negro during the Reconstruction years. After tracing the continuous pressure of the abolitionists upon the "timid government" of President Lincoln, he forecast the extent and nature of Negro adjustment and the prospect for post-Reconstruction agriculture and labor.

Even Tavares Bastos, inside Brazil, transmitted approvingly the Reclus expectation of the Negro as a free, skilled farm laborer. Both anticipated that the Negro was capable of great productivity after Reconstruction and freedom. This would not only maintain the stricken southern cotton plantation and factory, it would also contribute to the order and prosperity of both the Negro and all the people.

Not everyone shared this view. Slaveowners in Brazil blamed and dreaded the impact of emancipation upon them. When the Agassiz Expedition was in Rio de Janeiro, the professor one day noted the effect of the North American experience upon Brazilian slavery. In Chapter II of his *Journey in Brazil*, "Rio de Janeiro and Its Environs," with a subtitle "Ef-

fect of Emancipation in United States upon Slavery in Brazil,"
Professor Agassiz himself felt that Brazilians were trying to
achieve by gradualism that "which was forced upon us without political preparation." He wrote that if, politically, slavery
in Brazil was more "hopeful," from a moral point of view, it
looked more odious than in the United States. He noted that
because of poor religious instruction, Negro morals and sex
habits were bad, especially in Bahia.

The ramification of emancipation, contemporaries believed,
reached into Brazilian slavery. Agassiz tells how "Captain
Bradbury asked the proprietor . . . whether he hired or
owned his slaves. 'Own them — a hundred and more; but it
will finish soon,' he answered in his broken English. 'Finish
soon! How do you mean?' 'It finish with you, and when it finish with you, it finish here, it finish everywhere'. He said it
not in any tone of regret or complaint, but as an inevitable
fact. The death-note of slavery in the United States was its
death note everywhere. We thought this significant and
cheering."

The celebrated British consul, traveler, and writer, Richard
Burton, explored the "highlands of Brazil." He found this
feeling clear and strong. As he visited the different slaveowning areas, he concluded, from his talks with planters, "The
news reaching them from the United States are not suited for
calming them, and their importance guarantees the country's
consideration. Their attitude is legitimate since this highly
intelligent class will be the first to welcome the arrival of
white worker [i.e., immigrants]."

Writing something of an editorial on the emancipation of
the slaves, José Rodrigues wrote in his *O Novo Mundo* in 1870
that, "Four years ago, when Dom Pedro 2^0 declared he was
going to take measures to abolish the servile element in the
Empire as soon as possible, all the foreign press exulted with
sincere rejoicing to see Brazil receiving so quickly the moral
of the Civil War in the United States." As he saw it, he not

only saw the impact of the United States upon Brazil, but, in his inter-American way, he also expected that the Emperor would take steps as soon as possible to emancipate the slaves. Rodrigues lived well past the 1888 action, when Brazil did get around to it. Antislavery, according to Rodrigues, gave Brazil and the United States something in common: their struggle for civil liberty and human equality.

Rodrigues, like Tavares Bastos and Reclus, would have assured the planters about the flight of the Negro after freedom. Rodrigues repeatedly stressed the experience of the United States, under the protection of Reconstruction, as being opposed to flight and exodus. He did not want to go on record as asking too much too soon for the Brazilian Empire. Political gains had to keep step with economic and vocational ones.

In Brazil especially the slaveowners faced grimly the darkening cloud of abolition upon their horizon. Each slaveowning generation since Independence had seen with fear the gradual abolition of slavery: on the continent around them and then in nearby Guiana and in the Caribbean to their northeast. First came abolition in Spanish America, beginning with Independence and slowly extending until it reached Caribbean Colombia in 1853. Then followed abolition in the British Caribbean in Jamaica and Guiana in 1833; the great work of the French *Société des Amis des Noirs* culminated in the propaganda of Schoelcher in the French Caribbean. Slavery was abolished in Martinique and Guadeloupe in 1848. Since the revolt in Saint-Domingue (Haiti), the handwriting had been on the wall for New World slave masters; even Brazil was there. Only Cuba remained slave.

The abolitionist campaign in the United States, and the final capstone of the Emancipation Proclamation, added to the fears of planters, especially those with very large slaveholdings. The consequences of emancipation were far more serious than the idea or principle. Apparently the economic and financial loss was seen in terms of an abrupt and disastrous runaway of the emancipated slaves. Emancipation and abolition meant the immediate and wholesale extension of the *quilombo* (runaway slave community) and the economic desertion of the planter's labor force. This meant ruin to sugar, cotton, coffee, and tobacco plantations. The curious fact that the reverse tended to take place, that the slave stayed in the planter's vicinity, and that, in contrast, Confederate slave-owners did the migrating to Brazil, only brought home the fact that emancipation meant an uprooting, not a liberation or an abolition. The psychic image of the term "emancipation" to planters meant a deracination, an upset, a breakup of their economic power as masters and of their paternal way of life.

Other opinions in Brazil found a way of meeting their own needs and of avoiding the error of putting all of Brazil's slavery together. Tavares Bastos saw differences between slavery in the interior provinces, the coastal provinces, and those along Brazil's borders. He proposed immediate freedom, with compensation to owners, for slaves in those Brazilian provinces which adjoined the free states of Latin America. While this meant a different treatment for slaves near Guiana than for those near Argentina, he wanted to avoid the turmoil created by the Paraguayan War. In other states he applied the principle of gradualism and indemnization. His fine Brazilian federalism and sense of state and regional difference this time limited the influence and example of the United States only to an inspiration.

Brazilian geography and her enclavement among culturally different neighbors made it necessary to think of abolition in terms of war and imperialism, as well as federalism or freedom. Tavares Bastos wrote his views in a letter to the Secretary of the British and Foreign Anti-Slavery Society. There, he revealed his nationalism as well as his liberalism: that slavery along the border was a danger to Brazilian security, an element leading to military adventures. A Brazilian first, he passed even the lofty principle of antislavery through the fine mesh screen of national interest. In this he showed, as cultural diffusion, borrowing, and impact have shown almost everywhere, that one culture borrows basically in terms of its own. The impact of emancipation and Reconstruction upon Brazil was not total or automatic. Brazilian federalism and liberalism felt its impact but modified its stimulus to the energy level of Brazil.

Tavares Bastos reminded his Brazilian readers that in the United States, now so celebrated for the federal government's emancipation of 1863, it was the states who first abolished slavery. The states of the North and West did it historically, at different times. Consequently, as a realist and gradualist, he advised that abolition could not be simultaneous in Brazil. At best it could be immediate, or in a short time, in many of the provinces.

But what of the consequences of emancipation as well as the emancipation? Taking his cue from the report of the American Freedmen's Union as annexed to the Report of the Anti-Slavery Conference, he was particularly concerned with what the United States was doing to hold the Negroes to their birthplaces. He found that the freed slaves provided the working class where they had been raised. He almost raised his voice: let Brazil's states take notice and not forget it. To make a man of the slave the American makes him go to school. In Brazil the states controlled basic education, and Tavares Bastos brought the second American Revolution home to his "home-rule" people. "The world has never seen such a revolution, in the same society, in half a dozen years." Schools for all, child and adult, that was it! For the liberal Tavares Bastos, in a country which still has the highest illiteracy in Latin America, the remedy for society and education was schools for all. Abolition, emancipation, and the establishment of liberty through education were one and the same thing.

He praised the wartime protection of the freed slaves by the United States Army, followed by the work of the Freedmen's Union (a lay body) and the Freedmen's Bureau of the government. The presence of private initiative and personal effort was well known to him, but the Brazilian had no local equivalent of the Peabody Fund. The connection of North American white philanthropy and generosity with Negro education, science, liberty, and society made no impact upon Latin America until the twentieth century. The combination of American private sources, government aid, and public progress made an impression upon Tavares Bastos and many other Brazilians (and Latins).

What contemporaries see is not what later historians see. Sources are one thing for the beginning of a period; the historian of a hundred years later either uses sources which contemporaries did not know, or he interprets what they knew in the light of his own century.

What very few then saw, or now know, was the historical fact that Latin America drew its post-1870 (and even earlier) antislavery legislation from its own as well as outside experiences. The experiences of Spain and Portugal always influenced the history of their American colonies. Slavery and the effects of the North American Reconstruction era were not to be exceptions. Portuguese legal traditions and institutions were always strong in Brazil; Spain's were equally enduring in Spanish America.

This generalization holds as a specific for Latin America. The example of the Emancipation Proclamation did not take hold. Only the excitement over the action stirred emotions and enthusiasms. Nevertheless, the generation of Reconstruction, like the generation of present-day historians, believed that the action of Lincoln paved the way for Latin America.

It was probably the Colombian, Salvador Camacho Roldán, who first drew this connection. In his little book on Abraham Lincoln, which was translated from *La Opinión*, Bogotá, June 7, 1865, Camacho Roldán understood the greatness of Lincoln in raising the military and industrial might of the United

States. Indeed, he was the rare example of one Latin American who admired the wealth of the United States. He hoped the Colombian society would grow that way.

Several other Latin Americans of those days knew, as well as Karl Marx did, that the Civil War would result in the evolution of a North American capitalism. Latin Americans, like Camacho Roldán and others, knew very well that the bonds of North American society were being broken into atoms by the advent of a new civilization under the same Constitution. He praised Lincoln's common sense, his skill in drawing "generals from obscurity," and his ability in controlling the most colossal civil war of modern times.

But in his view of Lincoln's impact on slavery in Latin America, Camacho Roldán saw the emancipation as one of the great Inter-American doctrines. He referred to the tragic death of "Mr. Lincoln . . . a man . . . who freed four millions of slaves and prepared the way for freedom for the three millions more in the Spanish colonies and Brazil, and inaugurated the era of universal emancipation of the races, the regeneration even of Africa itself, of that great continent which is the affront of the century, will be perhaps one of the consequences of the abolition of slavery in North America. . . ."

Of course, the facts of history show that Portugal had an antislavery tradition too, which Brazil took over. The eighteenth-century role of Pombal, the powerful Portuguese minister, is in this direction. Taking the feudal principle of *stadtluft macht frei* and applying it to the European mother country, Pombal not only ended slavery within Portugal, he also prevented slaves from being taken there. If I am not mistaken, the notion that free soil provided freedom is a forerunner of the petition in both the eighteenth-century Somersett and the nineteenth-century Dred Scott cases. Then, later, the Portuguese and Spanish liberals advanced the additional concept that not only free soil in the mother country, but also in the womb of the mother, provides freedom.

Sá de Bandeira, the Portuguese mid–nineteenth-century liberal minister, laid the basis for emancipation in Angola by declaring all slaves free at birth. This was exactly the step of emancipation which Rio Branco of Brazil followed in 1871, and not the emancipation doctrine of Lincoln and North America. Yet Brazilians of that day looked to the United States for their example. Tavares Bastos, José Carlos Rodrigues, and the greatest abolitionist of all, Joaquim Nabuco, found the North American experience and model more real than the Portuguese. For Tavares Bastos on the Amazon, Joaquim Nabuco in Rio de Janeiro, and José Carlos Rodrigues in New York, the Reconstruction, with its Thirteenth and Fourteenth amendments, and the Freedmen's Bureau were concrete incentives to their own actions in Brazil, even though the cabinet of Rio Branco located other ideas. Finally, Brazil also had its experienced Negro troops, fighting in their own regiments, even as slaves. The loyalty of these veterans to officers and an empire in a country rich with the record of Negro *quilombo*-runaways provided a historic experience of its own, under obligation neither to the neighbor in the United States nor to its parent in Portugal.

The Civil War decade, and particularly the Reconstruction era in both the United States and Mexico, brought a rush of promoters, businessmen, speculators, investors, and managers. An "invasion" of Mexico took place after 1867 in a way not even Horace Greeley had advocated. Newspaper and public opinion in the United States had kept the interests of Americans in Mexico at a high pitch. Spanish language newspapers and magazines appeared. One of them, forerunner of present-day *Life International*, was Frank Leslie's *Illustrated Weekly*, in Spanish, for the Mexican market. Leslie's weekly in Spanish, the *Semanario Ilustrado*, was said to be one of the most widely read in Mexico. It was full of pictures and articles. It cast into Mexico a picture of the North American Reconstruction similar to that which *O Novo Mundo* was showing in

Portuguese for Brazil. Many Mexicans, Brazilians, and Colombians like Camacho Roldán hoped that the prosperity and production system of North American capitalism under the Reconstruction might be a model for Latin America. Reconstruction might also show them how to end their feudalism.

As I have written in a recent essay on the "Civil War and Latin America" (*The Impact Series*, ed. Allan Nevins and Harold Hyman [New York, in press]), the decades after 1865 really forced to the surface vital issues with real impact upon Latin America. South America had to notice them. The migration of American business and capital into Latin America has been going on for a century since. An industrial revolution was exported. So was the railway era. The ex-Army engineers with railway bridge-building experience in the Civil War, especially Army officers, were called on by Latin Americans to help survey and construct the lines in their countries. The Mexican Matías Romero knew and used this know-how for his country. The recently located papers of Hiram Barney, influential Republican lawyer of New York State, reveal how the process went on. The rural-village image of early America was changed by the Industrial Revolution.

The export of surplus engineers and businessmen added to the new, Reconstruction-derived image of "Yankee materialism." The view of power and technology fixed for a long time the South American notion of the United States. The other side of the same coin came from South American travelers to North America. They saw with unpleasant surprise the crowded, noisy streets, the wretched slums, the bewildered and lowly immigrant. Both sides of the coin represented the new money and the new rich. The sensitive Latin Americans noticed and complained of all this. This was no longer rural, no longer democratic. What they saw was plutocratic and the power of the new rich.

For Latin Americans, the Reconstruction also proved the power of nationalism and centralism, as well as the victory over states' rights. That is probably why the Federalist-Hamiltonian view of Professor Francis Lieber of Columbia College was put into Spanish translation. The power of federal government to prevent and crush state secession and separatism had been hailed by the Argentine Juan Alberdi. Victorious nationalism had many friends. Moreover, the political party which won North American nationalism would also help preserve the national and territorial integrity of the Latin American countries. So Matías Romero thought in Mexico. Neither the new North American corporation nor the new North American nation wanted to annex Latin American nationality.

Moreover, the Republican party sent out its own image. The Brazilians sought to use United States federalism as their model and many republicans opposed to the Empire were stimulated by North American republicanism. In addition, in Mexico, Matías Romero, that most Yankee of nineteenth-century Mexicans, helped found a Liberal party modeled on the American party system. He liked the convention system of nominations. Of course, he had close feeling and close connection with the post-Reconstruction Republican party in the United States. It is not surprising that he wanted to take the party into Mexico as a model, as he wanted to take North American capital into Mexico.

Neither the slavery nor the political view of the Reconstruction lasted too long. The economic and financial side took the limelight. Only in the first few years of the Reconstruction did Latin America take any notice of the Negro and his adjustment to freedom. The Negro became the forgotten man in the inter-American scene; the Indian and European immigrant took his place. There are exceptions to this, as usual. When the Brazilian Negro, André Rebouças, visited the United States, José Carlos Rodrigues made him acquainted with the work of Frederick Douglass. But politics and civil liberty went their separate ways, while trade and finance were getting together.

Nevertheless, slavery was only one basic factor in shaping the North American image during Reconstruction years. Public schools, libraries, the Homestead Act, and America as a melting pot were additional attractions and won attention, notice, and admiration. The Reconstruction, in fact, sent out many forms of energy which radiated into the Western hemisphere. Even Pan-American ideas came forward during those years, with early proposals for an association of nations. But the idea of a strengthened Negro helped by a strong nationalism was most appealing to Latin American liberalism and nationalism between 1865 and 1870. They looked long and hard at these colors in the North American portrait. Afterward what they saw was not pretty.

CANADA AND RECONSTRUCTION, 1863-79

W. L. MORTON
University of Manitoba

Canada in 1863 was one colony of several in what was then termed British North America. That was the territory of the Canada of today. United Canada, as it was then called, was the valley of the St. Lawrence, between the American frontier and the height of land to the north, and from the Straits of Belle Isle to Fort William on Lake Superior. To the east lay the Maritime Provinces of New Brunswick, Nova Scotia, Prince Edward Island, and Newfoundland. To the north and west lay the vast reaches of Rupert's Land — not a colony except for Selkirk's settlement on the Red River — and the Indian territory which bordered on Russian America. In the Pacific slope were the colonies of British Columbia and Vancouver Island. Self-governing within the British Empire, these small, scattered provinces of British North American had no real connection with one another except that which the Empire itself gave. That was then little enough, because the responsible government given the colonies in 1849 to 1855 was frankly regarded as a preparation for at least practical independence in due course. Colonial governors still came from Britain, and a steady flow of dispatches from the Colonial Office, but the British garrisons which were the visible mark of Empire had been cut to little more than token size in Canada, and even at that were grudged.

The "provinces" then, as their neighbors of "the states" called them, had little union among themselves. In Canada, most populous and wealthy of the colonies, the union imposed in 1840 had been under growing attack since 1851. Communities, so small in themselves, so scattered geographically, and so fiercely attached as they were to their new self-government, could hardly deal with the possible consequences of the tremendous convulsion which had torn its southern neighbor apart in civil war. The one unifier and defender they had, as the Trent crisis of 1861 had shown, was the United Kingdom. But the Trent crisis had also emphasized what was well known, that the United Kingdom had in the British North American colonies a military and naval liability it would be embarrassing to have to meet if the balance of power in Europe, or Asia, should be upset when that in America was also in question.

For it was impossible for Canada, or the United Kingdom, or any other power, to see the American Civil War as a conflict over merely constitutional, moral, or social issues. What was at issue, it was sensed, if not clearly seen, in Quebec, London, Paris, and St. Petersburg, if not in Washington, was that the war would end either in the division of the United States, or in its reconstruction as a more powerful state than it had hitherto been. If the division were confirmed, there would arise in the Americas a balance of power resembling that among the European powers, and one in which those powers would have to intervene. If, on the contrary, the union were to be reconstructed, then the position sketched in the Monroe Doctrine would be consolidated. There would be only one great power in the Americas, and no balance of power. National independence there might be for other states in the Americas, but there would be no military counterweight to the weight of the United States, and no European or Asian state might hope to intervene in American affairs against American opposition, at least in North America.

In either case, the inhabitants of the provinces to the north could only view the future with trepidation, unless they were, as a good number were, middle-class Protestants of liberal persuasion who regarded power politics as delusions of kings and European governments from which Victorian England and the United States were fortunately free. Such could and did favor the cause of the North and look to its victory with satisfaction and complacency. But to the conservatively minded, and the more "realistic," the struggle to the south could be viewed only as a struggle for power in which the provinces might become involved. The provinces, it seemed to them, faced grave alternatives. In a continent balanced between a truncated Union and a victorious but precariously placed South, the provinces would have faced embarrassing choices in trade, defense, and their political future. In one dominated by a victorious Union of military temper and military power, they might well face, so the more conservative feared, diplomatic pressure or even military aggression. Whichever the event, they could scarcely deal successfully with a neighbor so powerful and dynamic.

Neither of these alternatives was, of course, a matter of clear perception, still less of necessary choice, in 1863. Men lived then as now with only an imperfect grasp on what was actually happening in their times. But some matters were clear and pressing. One was that the war could not be ignored. It dominated the news in Canada as in the United States for four long years. It was impossible to be indifferent to it, and Canadians were not. Its issues, federal union, the rights of minorities and majorities, sectional struggles over economic policies, slavery — all these, especially the latter — were known and discussed in Canadian homes. Broadly speaking, Canadians strongly desired the abolition of slavery — it had, of course, completely ended in the provinces with imperial abolition in 1833 — and on the assumption that it was what the war was about, favored the northern cause at first. Many, like George Brown, never doubted that the war would destroy slavery and vindicate democracy. But the more conservative saw the war as a struggle for power between Canada's old allies, the southern states, and the power-grasping "Yankees" of the North. They favored the South, in their hearts, if not openly, and some hoped for a southern victory as a check on the North as late as the presidential election of 1864. For that main reason, and because of various irritations of the war, by the end of the war the prevailing popular sentiment in Canada was anti-northern.

Whatever sympathies or antipathies the provincials cherished, however, and whatever the views of the various governments of the British American provinces, the Civil War had practical effects upon colonial defense and upon border relations with the United States. Defense had indeed been an issue between the United Kingdom and the colonies for a decade.[1] The imperial government was more and more inclined to insist that local self-government meant local self-defense by militias locally equipped and paid. Imperial defense would, of course, remain an imperial responsibility, but all garrisons except that of the great naval base of Halifax would be withdrawn. Such measures would have meant a loss of cash and an increase of expenditure to the colonial governments, together with a loss of social tone and prestige in the garrison towns. The only war to which the colonies could be exposed, many of their politicians argued, would be one be-

---

[1] C. P. Stacey, in *Responsible Government and the British Army, 1849–1871* (Toronto, 1963), is the established authority in this field.

tween the Empire and the United States. As that would be none of their making, it would be an imperial war in which the Empire would be bound to defend them. The argument went on inconclusively until in 1855 and 1856 the Crimean War led to the slow beginnings of reform of the colonial militias. This was quickened by the war alert caused by the Franco-Austrian War in 1859. But it took the outbreak of war in the United States and the Trent affair both to bring British reinforcements and to lead to the serious reform of the colonial militias, particularly those of Canada and Nova Scotia. When Reconstruction began in 1863, the colonies were taking their defense seriously and could see clearly both the possibility of British withdrawal from the trap of an American war and the advantages of central control of defense. The Canadian Army in some sense is thus one of the by-products of the Civil War and Reconstruction.

Border relations were equally sobering and equally forced the pace of governmental growth in the colonies. The Canadian-American border unites even more than it divides. It divides, however, much more than usual when one country is at war and the other at peace. Not only did it lead to an increased flow of trade in 1863, as the demands of war sent American purchasers into the provinces in search of horses, fodder, and foodstuffs; it also led to an extraordinary multiplication of American consuls in the provinces whose duties included that of keeping an eye on southern agents and sympathizers in Canada. Recruiting agents plied their illegal trade, and Canadians all too often joined the fugitive ranks of "bounty-jumpers." Unwanted border crossings multiplied as the provinces became a haven for escaped Confederate prisoners of war. The Canadian response was to create a small body of stipendiary magistrates under the direction of the two attorney generals. Their duties were to furnish information from the border cities on the activities of Confederates and their sympathizers. Released at the end of the war, the magistrates were put to work again at once to deal with Fenian conspiracies. As a result they led to the formation of the Confederation of the Dominion Police, a small, informal F.B.I., which was merged with the Royal Canadian Mounted Police in 1920. The character of that force is now much more that of the original police force than that of a special police for the waste areas of Canada. The federal police of Canada thus owe their beginnings in part to Reconstruction.

Even more fundamental than the growth of the agencies of state was that of economic nationalism in Canada. Since 1855 the trade of the province had flowed not only east to the United Kingdom by the old channels, but also to the south by the new ones made by the Reciprocity Treaty. The provinces prospered partly in consequence, and probably the North at war was served by this trade. But the Republican victory in 1860 had been, among other things, a victory for economic nationalism, of the northern desire for protection over southern insistence on low tariffs. In Canada also there were the beginnings of industrialization and a desire for protection, despite a strong and general wish to maintain reciprocity. The end of the war, with a desperate South seeking to use the provinces to create a diversion from the final northern assault on the South, as in the St. Alban's Raid of 1864, played into the hands of the interests opposed to a continuation, or a renewal, of the treaty. After renewal for one year, it was terminated in 1866. The trade of the provinces was injured, but the movement toward confederation strengthened economic nationalism in Canada. The roots of the later National Policy are to be found in the economic character of Reconstruction and the submergence of low tariff sentiment in the United States by the subjugation of the South.

Underlying all these attitudes and changes was the realization, even by some of the Canadians who favored the northern cause and desired its victory, that Canada could not ignore the war and might suffer from it. The provinces, it came to be seen, had not only to prepare themselves by defense measures concerted with the United Kingdom, but also had to make an assertion of nationhood that the United States might respect in its own right. There was also the need to avoid being drawn into the struggle by the combatants themselves. This need, made urgent by the St. Alban's Raid, led to the passage of the Alien Act, similar to the acts suspending habeas corpus in Ireland, which gave the government of Canada (not of the other provinces) unexampled powers to arrest and hold suspects without trial.[2]

Behind the fears of conquest, which were little more than nightmares of wartime, was the fear of annexation. This, like conquest, was an old bugaboo of Canadian history. But there was some threat behind the outbursts urging annexation of the provinces, chiefly in the press of New York and St. Paul. One center of annexation sentiment, if it may be expressed so simply, was New York. So far as there was such sentiment, it reflected New York's old desire to draw into its hinterland all the country of the Great Lakes, to the detriment of Montreal and Boston. It reflected still more the grandiose views of William H. Seward, Secretary of State in both Lincoln's and Johnson's administrations. Seward himself was the most amiable of annexationists and never intended the provincials anything but good. But the pens of the editorial writers of the Seward press in New York city and state were more virulent, and their sporadic cries for annexation could be alarming, and could be used, in Canada.

Still another and more determined center of annexation was St. Paul, Minnesota. The trade with Red River since 1844 had drawn attention northward. That extraordinary publicist, J. W. Taylor, had become convinced that the best railway route to the west coast lay through British territory, and his views had won the interest of a group of commercial and

---

[2] *Province of Canada: Statutes, 1865,* 28 Victoria, chap. 1.

political adventurers in St. Paul. At Washington their aims were guided by Senator Alexander Ramsey of Minnesota, and their lobbying done by Taylor himself after 1862, from a position as an agent of the Treasury. There he persistently advocated the acquisition by the United States of the British Northwest, and eventually in some curious combination of New England and northwestern railway interests wrote the bill for the annexation of the British provinces which Representative Nathaniel P. Banks of Massachusetts introduced into Congress in 1866.[3] It was only introduced, not proceeded with, and proved of no more effect than the resolution of the legislature of Minnesota in 1868 calling for the liberation of the people of the Northwest. The bill was not very serious stuff, even as a move in American domestic politics, but it indicated to Canadians the possibility of a destiny other than one of their own shaping.

Much more serious, if also quite fantastic, was the Fenian danger which from 1865 to 1871 kept the Canadian governments and militia on the alert. The general strategy of the Fenian Brotherhood was simply to attack Britain through Canada, and embroil the United States with the United Kingdom in the process. The threat was dangerous for two reasons. One was that the British provinces, like the United States, held thousands of recent Irish immigrants; some of these were Fenians. Their presence on Canadian soil created the possibility that a Fenian lodgment, made on Canadian soil by Irish veterans from the Union armies, might receive support from within Canada. The danger proved to be slight, but it nevertheless existed. The other reason was that American officials might, in deference to the Irish vote which was important in the elections of 1866 and 1868, be slow in preventing the abuse of American neutrality by the launching of an invasion from American soil. They were to be slow by several days in 1866,

---

[3] See the author's *The Critical Years* (Toronto, 1965), p. 231.

but the British regulars and the Canadian militia, despite its defeat by Fenian invaders at Ridgeway, were adequate to meet the situation. In 1871 American official action was prompt, and the Fenian attempt to invade the new and restless province of Manitoba ended when American cavalry arrested the invaders as they prepared to cross the border. Whether Fenianism can be called an effect of Reconstruction is doubtful, but there was a connection with Reconstruction because the Irish were prone to vote Democrat, and could not be offended before elections by a Republican administration.

It is apparent, then, that Reconstruction forced an enormous growth of governmental activity and of economic nationalism in Canada. It was, in fact, one of the principal causes of Canadian Confederation, just as the War of Independence created the possibility of modern Canada. It is true, of course, that the roots, the dynamic forces, that made confederation are to be found within in the history of the British provinces themselves.[4] But the assurance of southern defeat after Gettysburg and the beginning of Reconstruction were the chief external pressures forcing the provinces, with many reasons for reluctance, toward political union.

Reconstruction, however, acted not only directly, but also indirectly, upon the growth and union of the provinces. It had, for example, reinforced the earlier pressure for the training of an embodied militia capable of taking the field. Yet such local defense forces were designed to fight under British command around British regular forces. From 1862 to 1864, for example, battalions of the Guards were in Canada for the second time in its history. This was a deliberate as well as unexampled commitment of British military prestige to the defense of Canada. Behind them was the disposable military and naval force of the Empire, so far as it was not,

---

[4] D. G. Creighton, "The United States and Canadian Confederation," *Canadian Historical Review*, XXXIX (September, 1958), 209–22.

or might not be, tied down in Europe and Asia. There could be no Canadian-American war, only a British-American one. From the Crimean War at least, and very sharply after the Danish-German War in 1864, British military and official opinion saw Canada as a military liability from which it was necessary to free the Empire. Yet the retreat must be a dignified one, and not harmful to imperial prestige. This could be done only by putting the colonies in a political and military posture that the United States would accept and respect. This could only be done by assisting in a political union of the colonies, and by the withdrawal of British troops from the interior of the continent in the valley of the St. Lawrence.[5] From this thinking came the prompt acceptance by the British government of the plan for confederation adopted by the Quebec Conference in October, 1864.

No doubt, also, the British government later took note of General U. S. Grant's very free comments when in August, 1865, he rather oddly spent a few days of a much needed holiday in Quebec. Grant said publicly as well as privately that Canadians had nothing to fear if Britain refrained from supporting Maximilian in Mexico, on the border of which, and not of Canada, he had, he said, placed 200,000 troops.[6] In short, Canada was safe if not a military menace to the United States. From such considerations came as well the unusual pressure on New Brunswick and Nova Scotia to enter a union which the voters of the former had once rejected in 1866, as those of the latter were to do in 1867. Canadian Confederation was one British reaction to Reconstruction.

There was still another indirect effect of Reconstruction on

---

[5] It was, of course, increasingly realized that the Province of United Canada was indefensible above Montreal. This was the gist of the two reports by Colonel W. F. O. Jervois in 1864.

[6] Archives des Affaires Etrangères, 37 (27) French Consul to Ministre des Affaires Etrangères, August 9, 1865; Quebec *Morning Chronicle*, August 6, 11, 1865.

Canadian Confederation. That was the extension of Canada to the Pacific between 1867 and 1871. There was general agreement among most Canadian political leaders that political union of the provinces alone would not assure an independent future for them. A West, a continental destiny, was necessary also. And it was indeed a fundamental element of the curious alchemy of Canadian Confederation that Canada could not expand eastward unless it also expanded westward, or westward unless eastward. In terms of railways, there could be no confederation without the Intercolonial Railway to the Atlantic, and no Intercolonial without the Pacific railway to the west. Ontario, the wealthiest province, would not pay for the Intercolonial unless it received in return the railway to the Pacific. Without the latter, moreover, the Northwest would fall to the reconstructed United States, and the new confederation, hived in the valley of the St. Lawrence, would stagnate, crumble, and drift into annexation. The acquisition of the West was a necessary part of confederation, and Reconstruction might have prevented that acquisition.

Reconstruction, then, was the catalyst which precipitated the crystallization of the elements making for union in the British provinces. It was so first because of the pressures Reconstruction put upon the provinces directly. But indirectly it was also the catalyst because of the reactions in Britain and the new dominion to the new power structure emerging in the Americas after 1863. Gettysburg was high tide of the Confederacy; its ebbing waters set the tide running that on Canadian shores was to bring in confederation.

The Dominion of Canada of 1867 was, then, a response, among other things, to Reconstruction. The dominion made a British withdrawal from the interior of North America possible for the first time since 1760. It created the idea of a Canadian nationality which might claim American respect, however odd, however revolutionary, the manner of its birth. It might create a viable economy that would support political independence. In forming the new union, Canadian statesmen, led by John A. Macdonald, created very much that kind of stronger central government, the lack of which, as they saw, had led to the war, and which the politicians of Reconstruction created. And they chose to make the new union in a distinctive way, a slightly dangerous way in the times. The new nation, as it proudly called itself, was to be, though federal, not republican but monarchical, and its government, though democratic, was to be not congressional but parliamentary. Denied by British discretion the title of kingdom and the appointment of a viceroy as its head, it was still a kingdom in substance. The response to Reconstruction was made in British and Canadian terms, a cause of some criticism south of the border. To have an upstart kingdom appear in the north just as a tinsel empire tinkled to the ground in Mexico would indeed have been trying to the vindicated republic.

Whatever its form of government, however, the dominion was created among other things to carry out the necessary annexation of the Northwest, the vast territories of the Hudson's Bay Company, and to unite with the province of British Columbia. The Northwest would provide a route for the railway to the Pacific. It would give a new area of settlement, desperately needed in the Canadas, on the prairie lands. It would give the new dominion a frontage on the Pacific. The whole would be a continental destiny of its own for the new nation. That destiny was nearly thwarted, however, by a local revolt, and would have been had the United States chosen to intervene.

The actual negotiations with the Hudson's Bay Company and the colony of British Columbia went well enough, again owing to the support of the British government. That enormously realistic wielder of power was determined not only to withdraw from the possibility of continental entanglement with a reconstructed United States, but as a corollary to make Canada the legatee of all its North American holdings. The hitch that was to occur, and to throw open the possibility of intervention by a United States which had purchased Alaska in 1867 and which might respond to pressure from Minnesota, was caused by the action of an unregarded factor, the *métis* of Red River. The resistance by this handful of buffalo hunters and tripmen, led by Louis Riel, to the transfer in 1869 of the territory to Canada without terms with the people of the territory succeeded easily because of the remoteness of Red River from Ottawa and the lateness of the season that made any movement of troops impossible until the following summer. Before that happened, intervention by Americans, or even the American government, would have easily been possible. And the pushing of annexation by Oscar Malmros, the American vice-consul in Winnipeg, and by private members of the "American party" in Red River, was open and unabashed late in 1869.[7] Canada had therefore to try to keep the people of Red River quiet and to negotiate terms during the winter of 1869-70, in part at least to forestall an American intervention it was thought might be possible.

It would seem that such intervention, though not likely, was not impossible. There were real American interests involved. One was the "frontier" interest of St. Paul and Minnesota. The Red River territory had become in the previous twenty years a hinterland and an area of commercial expansion for Minnesota; the personal and commercial connections between St. Paul and Winnipeg were numerous and continuous. And the supporters of the Northern Pacific, who now included the great financier, Jay Cooke, were greatly interested in using, or at least controlling, the Canadian route to the Pacific. It was not surprising therefore that in April, 1870, a St. Paul exploring party, led by Colonel W. R. Marshall, visited Red River on behalf of Cooke. What they reported to

---

[7] *The Red River Journal of Alexander Begg*, ed. W. L. Morton (Toronto, 1957), pp. 8–9.

him Cooke reported to Grant, now President of the United States.[8]

The Grant administration was interested in the uprising in Red River. Hamilton Fish, as Secretary of State, took the precaution of dispatching J. W. Taylor to Ottawa as special agent on Red River affairs. He gave some thought to the spectacle of the people of Red River struggling to be free from tyrannical annexation to Canada.[9] Neither he nor the President were averse to using the trouble in Red River to induce Canada and Britain to be reasonable in other matters. Grant in particular, with his quiet obstinacy, was resolved that someday Britain's troubles would enable the United States to present "its little bill" for British policies during the Civil War.[10] Red River might have been the occasion.

It was not to be, however. As often in Canadian history, American interest in the Caribbean averted the possibility of pressure on Canada. Cuba and Santo Domingo were of more importance in 1870 than any difficulties with Canada, particularly over Red River. Canada, therefore, having come to terms with Red River in the Manitoba Act, which made the little settlement a province of the dominion, could send on its way in June, 1870, the Red River Expedition under Colonel Garnet Wolseley. The expedition contained a battalion of British regulars. The Grant administration might have refused permission to pass the expedition's supplies through the American canal at Sault Sainte Marie.[11] It agreed, after hesitation and debate, to do so, and Wolseley continued on his slow way by the old fur trade route from Fort William to Fort Garry. For the first time since the Oregon crisis, and for the

---

[8] *Ibid.*, pp. 127–28.

[9] J. W. Taylor Papers, Minnesota Historical Society Archives.

[10] Charles Sumner to John Bright, August 8, 1965, John Bright Papers, British Museum.

[11] Hamilton Fish Diary, May 14, 1870, United States National Archives.

last time, British troops were to stand their farthest west within North America. It was a long way to come, as a young officer remarked in his diary, to hear the band play "God Save the Queen." Yet it was imperative for the future of Canada that a symbol of imperial power should be shown by the troubled Red River. By this last, reluctant act of imperial policy in North America, Britain, with American acquiescence, assured to Canada the Northwest and a national future.

The union with British Columbia and the chartering of the Pacific railway, to be financed with loans guaranteed in the first place by the imperial treasury for building fortification around Montreal, completed the plans for uniting British North America. The United States, as a part of the reconstruction of its position in America, had accepted Canada as a continental neighbor.

This acceptance underlay the Treaty of Washington of 1871. The history of the origins and negotiations of that treaty have been repeatedly discussed in ever greater detail, and no attempt will be made to add to that detail here. Suffice it to say that the treaty was a vital part of Reconstruction in its external aspects. The treaty was, in fact, a peace settlement between the United States and Britain which concluded a war that wisely had never been fought. That peace settlement saw Britain accept, as Russia had accepted by the sale of Alaska, the supremacy of the United States in North America. The United States was therefore doubly free to proceed with the many aspects of Reconstruction, the continued effort to remodel the South and to make citizens of those who had recently been slaves, to complete the breaking of the Plains Tribes, and to exploit the West. And it fitted Canada into the new pattern of power in America.

To be accepted as a continental nation was in fact the vital thing for Canada. But the matter was not that simply stated at the time, and attention focused on detail. Nor was Canada accepted as a sovereign American nation; it was not such in law. It was therefore dealt with as part of an empire whose government was under domestic pressure and with which the United States felt free to bargain with closely. Canada therefore saw its interests sacrificed to the imperial interests in a settlement. Its inland navigation was traded for a *quid pro quo* in the extreme Northwest, never yet of any importance. It was allowed neither to control nor to bargain with its fisheries. It was not allowed to claim damages for the Fenian raids. In short, it had to settle its American difficulties as a new junior partner of a Britain embarrassed by the Alabama claims and the Russian violation of the Black Sea clauses of the Treaty of Paris, on the terms the United States saw fit to accept. By a final irony, the San Juan dispute, which by the treaty was submitted to arbitration, went against Canada and left its southern channel to the Pacific under the guns of American artillery. The limitations of semicolonial status, the international servitudes in the fisheries of colonial days, and the pressure the United States felt impelled to exercise on an imperial rival remained to circumscribe the aspirations of the new dominion. And by the rejection of reciprocity, the negotiators of the treaty made inevitable the further growth of economic nationalism in Canada.

Yet in the circumstances of the Reconstruction period these disabilities were slight. Perhaps the surprising thing is that the United States in the first days of its new power, while the war temper still smoldered and Anglo-Irish troubles inflamed Anglo-American relations, did not use that power to exact much instead of little. The reasons for this moderation were first, of course, the judicious and legal temper of Hamilton Fish. His moderate diplomacy, however, was possible because the interest of the United States was concerned with other matters.

The first of these was that in 1871 the British military hold on the St. Lawrence was ended when the last two battalions of British regulars marched down from the citadel of Quebec to the waiting troopships. Perhaps only military eyes such as Grant's took in the significance of that withdrawal, but it meant that the Canadian border was at long last undefended and that Canada would no more be, even symbolically, a military threat to American supremacy in America. American tourists on the Plains of Abraham would no longer hear the morning and evening bugles of the Empire on which in fact the sun had begun to set.

The undefended border was to become a system of mutual and restraining pressure as Canadian railways became alternatives to American lines. Each kept down the rates on the other, whatever the nationality of the goods they carried, whether they carried any or not. The fast-growing railway network of the continent did not ignore the boundary, but the rivalry of the inland sections and the ocean seaports kept the lines open to the competitive movement of goods and so created one of the new continental interests of the age of industrialization which Reconstruction established firmly in American life.

Nor did the United States really covet the Canadian West. The North had fought the Civil War in part, as the three preceding great wars of American history had been fought, to open the West. In Reconstruction it built the transcontinental railway that linked the East to the Pacific Coast. It carried forward the homesteading of the interior into the trans-Mississippi. Its once more small regular army was busy with the garrisoning of the South and with the Indian wars on the plains. The muscle, the brains, the money of the United States went into the building up of a new industrial East and a new agricultural West. Canada was left free to open its own West if it could.

The Canada of 1872 was confident that it could. In the general election of that year there was some talk of a National Policy, the answer to the American rejection of reciprocity from behind Reconstruction protective tariffs. On the crest of the boom then running Parliament chartered the Pacific railway. Then came the political crash of the Pacific Scandal and the economic crash of 1873.

The nation-building program thus crumbled, and Macdonald's Conservative party gave way to Alexander Mackenzie's Liberals, who were both the critics of that program and the inheritors of depression. Retrenchment, reform, and reciprocity were their remedies for political and economic ills. The latter, despite a hopeful beginning by George Brown, the long-time champion of the North and a warm friend of the United States, was refused by the economic nationalism of the same Reconstruction. Even a Liberal Canada had to walk the lonely path of nationalism.

A result of this rebuff, and also of the depression, was a rekindling in Canada of the fires of economic nationalism. At this fire John A. Macdonald, discredited by the Pacific Scandal, was able to warm his hands again, and, to mix the metaphor slightly, to soar phoenix-like from the ashes of political defeat. He and the Conservative party did so on the platform of the National Policy, a veiled but firm adoption of a policy of protective tariffs for Canadian industry. The tariff policy of the Reconstruction Republican party had helped to create in Canada a countering tariff policy and had made possible the completion of the Pacific railway and the building of the Canadian nation.[12]

To Reconstruction within the United States, Canadians gave little attention. The great decision of the Civil War had been made, and Reconstruction was its outcome. To that event they had had to adapt themselves, and had done so in the creation of the new dominion. But they then became in-

---

[12] The subject of Canadian economic policy in these years has been presented brilliantly in a fresh light by Robert Craig Brown in *Canada's National Policy, 1883–1900* (Princeton, N.J., 1964).

volved in their titanic task of making a viable state of their new, enormous, unexploited, and largely unknown empire. Like the United States, they turned inward. The abolition of slavery had, of course, been welcomed by Canadians, even if few realized, or even expected, that the ending of Negro slavery must lead to the equality of black and white men. The difficulties of black Reconstruction were viewed with indifference or with sympathy, according to temperament, but probably usually with a keen, practical awareness of the implications for the Republican and Democratic parties of that contest. There was now little sympathy for the defeated South, little romantic sympathy, that is, and none for the sinister forms of southern resistance, the Ku Klux Klan, or the Knights of the White Camellia. The old friend and rival, the United States, was stronger than ever, but not appreciably different. Canadian society acquired a good deal of the harshness, the arrogance, and the moral obtuseness of the Reconstruction temper, but this was the usual transborder influence, not a deliberate acceptance. It would seem that Canada was neither much aware of nor much affected by the social and human aspects of Reconstruction.

In summary, then, Canada had seen the United States reconstituted, established as the supreme power in the Americas where a balance of power was no longer possible, from which indeed Canada was to be blessedly absent, and set upon the course that was to lead to the present position of the United States in the world. Reconstruction had indeed been one, but only one, of the forces that had brought about confederation and created a Canadian nation with a continental destiny of its own, within the orbit of American power. Reconstruction had helped economic nationalism prevail in Canada over economic continentalism, and had led to the National Policy of 1879. It had, however, produced little change in the popular attitude of Canadians toward the United States as a government or toward American society. That was to come in the next century. For the balance of the nineteenth century Canada had to live with the America of Reconstruction, an America in many ways unsympathetic with its northern neighbor, although it helped it to grow and harden in the mold of nationalism as much by its economic policies as by its political acceptance.

As the Confederacy sank in the South, then, the Confederation arose in the north. Reconstruction subdued the southern states to the purposes of the Union. It accepted the northern provinces as a nation, because the new union fitted into the new hegemony in America which in external matters Reconstruction expressed and realized.

SEEDS OF FAILURE
IN RADICAL
RACE POLICY

C. VANN WOODWARD
Yale University

The Republican leaders were quite aware in 1865 that the issue of Negro status and rights was closely connected with the two other great issues of Reconstruction — who should reconstruct the South and who should govern the country. But while they were agreed on the two latter issues, they were not agreed on the first. They were increasingly conscious that in order to reconstruct the South along the lines they planned they would require the support and the votes of the freedmen. And it was apparent to some that once the reconstructed states were restored to the Union the Republicans would need the votes of the freedmen to retain control over the national government. While they could agree on this much, they were far from agreeing on the status, the rights, the equality, or the future of the Negro.

The fact was that the constituency on which the Republican congressmen relied in the North lived in a race-conscious, segregated society devoted to the doctrine of white supremacy and Negro inferiority. "In virtually every phase of existence," writes Leon Litwack with regard to the North in 1860, "Negroes found themselves systematically separated from whites. They were either excluded from railway cars, omnibuses, stagecoaches, and steamboats or assigned to special 'Jim Crow' sections; they sat, when permitted, in secluded and remote corners of theatres and lecture halls; they could not enter most hotels, restaurants, and resorts, except as servants; they prayed in 'Negro pews' in the white churches. . . . Moreover, they were often educated in segregated schools, punished in segregated prisons, nursed in segregated hospitals, and buried in segregated cemeteries." Ninety-three per cent of the 225,000 northern Negroes in 1860 lived in states that denied them the ballot, and 7 per cent lived in the five New England states that permitted them to vote. Ohio and New York had discriminatory qualifications that practically eliminated Negro voting. In many northern states discriminatory laws excluded Negroes from interracial marriage, from militia service, from the jury box, and from the witness stand when whites were involved. Ohio denied them poor relief, and most states of the old Northwest had laws carrying penalties against Negroes settling in those states. Everywhere in the free states the Negro met with barriers to job opportunities, and in most places he encountered severe limitations to the protection of his life, liberty, and property.[1]

One political consequence of these racial attitudes was that the major parties vied with each other in their professions of devotion to the dogma of white supremacy. Republicans were especially sensitive on the point because of their antislavery associations. Many of them, like Senator Lyman Trumbull of Illinois, the close friend of Lincoln, found no difficulty in reconciling antislavery with anti-Negro views. "We, the Re-

---

[1] Leon Litwack, *North of Slavery: The Negro in the Free States, 1790–1860* (Chicago, 1961), pp. 91–97.

publican party," said Senator Trumbull in 1858, "are the white man's party. We are for free white men, and for making white labor respectable and honorable, which it can never be when negro slave labor is brought into competition with it." Horace Greeley the following year regretted that it was "the controlling idea" of some of his fellow Republicans "to prove themselves 'the white man's party,' or else all the mean, low, ignorant, drunken, brutish whites will go against them from horror of 'negro equality.'" Greeley called such people "the one-horse politicians," but he could hardly apply that name to Lyman Trumbull, nor for that matter to William H. Seward, who in 1860 described the American Negro as "a foreign and feeble element like the Indians, incapable of assimilation"; nor to Senator Henry Wilson of Massachusetts, who firmly disavowed any belief "in the mental or the intellectual equality of the African race with this proud and domineering white race of ours."[2] Trumbull, Seward, and Wilson were the front rank of Republican leadership and they spoke the mind of the Middle West, the Middle Atlantic states, and New England. There is much evidence to sustain the estimate of W. E. B. Du Bois that "At the beginning of the [Civil] war probably not one white American in a hundred believed that Negroes could become an integral part of American democracy."[3]

As the war for union began to take on the character of a war for freedom, northern attitudes toward the Negro paradoxically began to harden rather than soften. This hardening process was especially prominent in the northwestern or middle western states where the old fear of Negro invasion was intensified by apprehensions that once the millions of slaves below the Ohio River were freed they would push northward — this time by the thousands and tens of thousands, perhaps

---

[2] Quoted in *ibid.*, pp. 92, 269–72.
[3] W. E. B. Du Bois, *Black Reconstruction in America, 1860–1880* (New York, 1935), p. 191.

in mass exodus, instead of in driblets of one or two who came furtively as fugitive slaves. The prospect of Negro immigration, Negro neighbors, and Negro competition filled the whites with alarm, and their spokesmen voiced their fears with great candor. "There is," Lyman Trumbull told the Senate, in April, 1862, "a very great aversion in the West — I know it to be so in my state — against having free negroes come among us. Our people want nothing to do with the negro."[4] And about the same time John Sherman, who was to give his name to the Radical Reconstruction Act five years later, told Congress that in Ohio "we do not like negroes. We do not disguise our dislike. As my friend from Indiana [Congressman Joseph A. Wright] said yesterday, the whole people of the northwestern states are, for reasons whether correct or not, opposed to having many negroes among them and the principle or prejudice has been engrafted in the legislation of nearly all the northwestern States."[5]

So powerful was this anti-Negro feeling that it almost overwhelmed antislavery feeling and seriously imperiled the passage of various confiscation and emancipation laws designed to free the slave. To combat the opposition Republican leaders such as George W. Julian of Indiana, Albert G. Riddle of Ohio, and Salmon P. Chase advanced the theory that emancipation would actually solve northern race problems. Instead of starting a mass migration of freedman northward, they argued, the abolition of slavery would not only put a stop to the entry of fugitive slaves but would drain the northern Negroes back to the South. Once slavery were ended, the Negro would flee northern race prejudice and return to his natural environment and the congenial climate of the South.[6]

One tentative answer of the Republican party to the north-

---

[4] Quoted in Jacque Voegeli, "The Northwest and the Race Issue, 1861–1862," *Mississippi Valley Historical Review*, L (1963), 240.

[5] *Congressional Globe*, 37 Cong., 2 Sess. (April 2, 1862), p. 1495.

[6] Voegeli, "The Northwest and the Race Issue," pp. 240–41.

ern fear of Negro invasion, however, was deportation of the freedmen and colonization abroad. The scheme ran into opposition from some Republicans, especially in New England, on the ground that it was inhumane as well as impractical. But with the powerful backing of President Lincoln and the support of western Republicans Congress overcame the opposition. Lincoln was committed to colonization not only as a solution to the race problem but as a means of allaying northern opposition to emancipation and fears of Negro exodus. To dramatize his solution the President took the unprecedented step of calling Negro leaders to the White House and addressing them on the subject. "There is an unwillingness on the part of our people," he told them on August 14, 1862, "harsh as it may be, for you free colored people to remain with us." He told them that "your race suffer very greatly, many of them by living among us, while ours suffer from your presence. . . . If this be admitted, it affords a reason at least why we should be separated."[7]

The fall elections following the Emancipation Proclamation were disastrous for the Republican party. And in his annual message in December the President returned to the theme of northern fears and deportation. "But it is dreaded that the freed people will swarm forth and cover the whole land," he said. They would flee the South, he suggested, only if they had something to flee from. "*Heretofore*," he pointed out, "colored people to some extent have fled North from bondage, and *now*, perhaps, from both bondage and destitution. But if gradual emancipation and deportation be adopted, they will have neither to flee from." They would cheerfully work for wages under their old masters "till new homes can be found for them in congenial climes and with people of their own blood and race." But even if this did not keep the Negroes

---

[7] *The Collected Works of Abraham Lincoln*, ed. Roy P. Bassler (New Brunswick, N.J., 1953), V, 371–72.

out of the North, Lincoln asked, "in any event, can not the North decide for itself whether to receive them?"[8] Here the President was suggesting that the northern states might resort to exclusion laws such as some of them used before the war to keep Negroes out.

During the last two years of the war northern states began to modify or repeal some of their anti-Negro and discriminatory laws. But the party that emerged triumphant from the crusade to save the Union and free the slave was not in the best political and moral position to expand the rights and assure the equality of the freedman. There undoubtedly *did* emerge eventually an organization determined to overthrow Andrew Johnson's states' rights, white-supremacy policies and to take over the control of the South. But that was a different matter. On the issue of Negro equality the party remained divided, hesitant, and unsure of its purpose. The historic commitment to equality it eventually made was lacking in clarity, ambivalent in purpose, and capable of numerous interpretations.* Needless to say, its meaning has been debated from that day to this.

The northern electorate the Republicans faced in seeking support for their program of Reconstruction had undergone no conversion in its wartime racial prejudices and dogmas. As George W. Julian, who deplored the fact himself, told his colleagues in the House in 1866, "the real trouble is that *we hate the negro*. It is not his ignorance that offends us, but his color."[9]

In the years immediately following the war every northern state in which the electorate or the legislature was given the opportunity to express its views on issues involving the poli-

---

[8] *Ibid.*, pp. 535–36.

[9] George W. Julian, *Speeches on Political Questions* (New York, 1872), p. 299.

*This admittedly represents a change from views earlier expressed on this subject by the author.

tical rights of the Negro reaffirmed its earlier and conservative stand. This included the states that reconsidered — and re-affirmed — their laws excluding Negroes from the polls. Five states with laws barring Negro testimony in court against whites repealed them, and a few acted against school segrega-tion. Throughout these years, however, the North remained fundamentally what it was before — a society organized upon assumptions of racial privilege and segregation. As Senator Henry Wilson of Massachusetts told his colleagues in 1867, "There is not today a square mile in the United States where the advocacy of the equal rights and privileges of those col-ored men has not been in the past and is not now unpopular."[10] Whether the senator was entirely accurate in his estimate of white opinion or not, he faithfully reflected the political con-straints and assumptions under which his party operated as they cautiously and hesitantly framed legislation for Negro civil and political rights — a program they knew had to be made acceptable to the electorate that Senator Wilson de-scribed.

This is not to suggest that there was not widespread and sincere concern in the North for the terrible condition of the freedmen in the South. There can be no doubt that many northern people were deeply moved by the reports of atroci-ties, peonage, brutality, lynchings, riots, and injustices that filled the press. Indignation was especially strong over the Black Codes adopted by some of the Johnsonian state legis-latures, for they blantantly advertised the intention of some southerners to substitute a degrading peonage for slavery and make a mockery of the moral fruits of northern victory. What is sometimes overlooked in analyzing northern response to the Negro's plight is the continued apprehension over the threat of a massive Negro invasion of the North. The panicky fear that this might be precipitated by emancipation had been al-

---

[10] *Congressional Globe*, 40 Cong., 3 Sess. (January 28, 1869) p. 672.

layed in 1862 by the promises of President Lincoln and other Republican spokesmen that once slavery were abolished the freedmen would cheerfully settle down to remain in the South, that northern Negroes would be drawn back to the South, and that deportation and colonization abroad would take care of any threat of northern invasion that remained. But not only had experiments with deportation come to grief, but southern white persecution and abuse combined with the ugly Black Codes had produced new and powerful incentives for a Negro exodus while removal of the shackles of slavery cleared the way for emigration.

The response of the Republican Congress to this situation was the Civil Rights Act of 1866, later incorporated into the Fourteenth Amendment. Undoubtedly part of the motivation for this legislation was a humanitarian concern for the protection of the Negro in the South, but another part of the motivation was concerned with the protection of the white man in the North. Senator Roscoe Conkling of New York, a member of the Joint Committee of Fifteen who helped draft the Civil Rights provisions, was quite explicit on this point. "Four years ago," he said in the campaign of 1866, "mobs were raised, passions were roused, votes were given, upon the idea that emancipated negroes were to burst in hordes upon the North. We then said, give them liberty and rights at the South, and they will stay there and never come into a cold climate to die. We say so still, and we want them let alone, and that is one thing that this part of the amendment is for."[11]

Another prominent member of the Joint Committee who had a right to speak authoritatively of the meaning of its racial policy was George Boutwell of Massachusetts. Addressing his colleagues in 1866 Boutwell said:

---

[11] Alfred R. Conkling, *The Life and Letters of Roscoe Conkling, Orator, Statesman, Advocate* (New York, 1889), p. 277.

I bid the people, the working people of the North, the men who are struggling for subsistence, to beware of the day when the southern freedmen shall swarm over the borders in quest of those rights which should be secured to them in their native states. A just policy on our part leaves the black man in the South where he will soon become prosperous and happy. An unjust policy [in the South] forces him from home and into those states where his rights will be protected, to the injury of the black man and the white man both of the North and the South. Justice and expediency are united in indissoluble bonds, and the men of the North cannot be unjust to the former slaves without themselves suffering the bitter penalty of transgression.[12]

The "bitter penalty" to which Boutwell referred was not the pangs of a Puritan conscience. It was an invasion of southern Negroes. "Justice and expediency" were, in the words of a more famous statesman of Massachusetts, "one and inseparable."

The author and sponsor of the Civil Rights Act of 1866 was Senator Lyman Trumbull, the same man who had in 1858 described the Republicans as "the white man's party," and in 1862 had declared that "our people want nothing to do with the negro." He had nevertheless fought for the Freedman's Bureau and civil rights in the South. Trumbull's bill was passed and after Johnson's veto was repassed by an overwhelming majority. Limited in application, the Civil Rights Act did not confer political rights or the franchise on the freedmen.

The Fourteenth Amendment, which followed, was also equivocal on racial questions and freedmen's rights. Rejecting Senator Sumner's plea for a guarantee of Negro suffrage, Congress left that decision up to the southern states. It also left northern states free to continue the disfranchisement of Negroes, but it exempted them from the penalties inflicted on

---

[12] Quoted in *The Journal of the Joint Committee of Fifteen on Reconstruction*, ed. Benjamin B. Kendrick (New York, 1914), pp. 341–42.

the southern states for the same decision. The real concern of the franchise provisions of the Fourteenth Amendment was not with justice to the Negro but with justice to the North. The rebel states stood to gain some twelve seats in the House if all Negroes were counted as a basis of representation and to have about eighteen fewer seats if none were counted. The amendment fixed apportionment of representation according to enfranchisement.

There was a great deal of justice and sound wisdom in the amendment, and not only in the first section conferring citizenship and protecting rights, but in the other three sections as well. No sensible person could contend that the rebel states should be rewarded and the loyal states penalized in apportionment of representation by the abolition of slavery and the counting of voteless freedmen. That simply made no sense. Nor were there many in the North at least who could object to the temporary disqualification for office and ballot of such southern officeholders of the old regime as were described in the third section. The fourth section asserting the validity of the national debt and voiding the Confederate debts was obviously necessary. As it turned out these were the best terms the South could expect — far better than it eventually got — and the South would have been wise to have accepted them.

The tragic failure in statesmanship of the Fourteenth Amendment lay in the equivocal and pusillanimous way it was presented. In equivocal deference to states' rights, the South was requested to approve instead of being compelled to accept. In this I think the moderates were wrong and Thaddeus Stevens was right. As W. R. Brock put it, "The onus of decision was passed to the Southern States at a moment when they were still able to defy Congress but hardly capable of taking a statesmanlike view of the future." [13] It was also the

---

[13] W. R. Brock, *An American Crisis: Congress and Reconstruction, 1865–1867* (London, 1963), p. 149.

fateful moment when President Johnson declared war on Congress and advised the South to reject the amendment. Under the circumstances it was inevitable that the South should reject it, and it did with stunning unanimity. Only thirty-two votes were cast for ratification in all the southern legislatures. This spelled the end of any hope for the moderate position in the Republican leadership.

After two years of stalling, of endless committee work and compromise, the First Reconstruction Act was finally adopted in the eleventh hour of the expiring Thirty-ninth Congress. Only after this momentous bill was passed was it realized that it had been drastically changed at the last moment by amendments that had not been referred to or considered by committees and that had been adopted without debate in the House and virtually without debate in the Senate. In a panicky spirit of urgency men who were ordinarily clearheaded yielded their better judgment to the demand for anything-is-better-than-nothing. Few of them liked what they got and fewer still understood the implications and the meaning of what they had done. Even John Sherman, who gave his name to the bill, was so badly confused and misled on its effect that he underestimated by some 90 per cent the number who would be disqualified from office and disfranchised. And this was one of the key provisions of the bill. It was, on the whole, a sorry performance and was far from doing justice to the intelligence and statesmanship and responsibility of the men who shaped and passed the measure.

One thing was at least clear, despite the charges of the southern enemies and the claims of the northern friends of the act to the contrary. It was not primarily devised for the protection of Negro rights and the provision of Negro equality. Its primary purpose, however awkwardly and poorly implemented, was to put the southern states under the control of men loyal to the Union or men the Republicans thought they could trust to control those states for their purposes. So far as the Negro's future was concerned, the votes of the Congress that adopted the Reconstruction Act speak for themselves. Those votes had turned down Stevens' proposal to assure an economic foundation for Negro equality and Sumner's resolutions to give the Negro equal opportunity in schools and in homesteads and full civil rights. As for the Negro franchise, its provisions, like those for civil rights, were limited. The Negro franchise was devised for the passage of the Fourteenth Amendment and setting up the new southern state constitutions. But disfranchisement by educational and property qualifications was left an option, and escape from the whole scheme was left open by permitting the choice of military rule. No guarantee of proportional representation for the Negro population was contemplated and no assurance was provided for Negro officeholding.[14]

A sudden shift from defiance to acquiescence took place in the South with the passage of the Reconstruction Act of March 2, 1867. How deep the change ran it would be hard to say. The evidence of it comes largely from public announcements of the press and conservative leaders, and on the negative side from the silence of the voices of defiance. The mood of submission and acquiescence was experimental, tentative, and precarious at best. It cannot be said to have predominated longer than seven months, from spring to autumn of 1867. That brief period was crucial for the future of the South and the Negro in the long agony of Reconstruction.

Southerners watched intently the forthcoming state elections in the North in October. They were expected to reflect northern reactions to radical Reconstruction and especially to the issue of Negro suffrage. There was much earnest speculation in the South. "It may be," said the Charleston *Mercury*, "that Congress but represents the feelings of its constituents,

---

[14]Seldon Henry, "Radical Republican Policy Toward the Negro" (unpublished Ph.D. dissertation, Yale, 1963), pp. 204–17.

that it is but the moderate mouthpiece of incensed Northern opinion. It may be that measures harsher than any . . . that confiscation, incarceration, banishment may brood over us in turn! But all these things will not change our earnest belief — that *there will be a revulsion of popular feeling in the North.*" [15]

Hopes were aroused first by the elections in Connecticut on April 1, less than a month after the passage of the Reconstruction Act. The Democrats won in almost all quarters. The radical *Independent* taunted the North for hypocrisy. "Republicans in all the great states, North and West, are in a false position on this question," it said. "In Congress they are for impartial suffrage; at home they are against it." In only six states outside the South were Negroes permitted to vote, and in none with appreciable Negro population. The *Independent* thought that "it ought to bring a blush to every white cheek in the loyal North to reflect that the political equality of American citizens is likely to be sooner achieved in Mississippi than in Illinois — sooner on the plantation of Jefferson Davis than around the grave of Abraham Lincoln!" [16] Election returns in October seemed to confirm this. Republican majorities were reduced throughout the North. In the New England states and in Nebraska and Iowa they were sharply reduced, and in New York, New Jersey, and Maryland the party of Reconstruction went down to defeat. Democrats scored striking victories in Pennsylvania and Ohio. In Ohio Republicans narrowly elected the governor by 8,000 votes but overwhelmed a Negro suffrage amendment by 40,000. In every state where the voters expressed themselves on the Negro suffrage issue they turned it down.

Horace Greeley read the returns bluntly, saying that "the

---

[15] Charleston *Mercury* quoted in DeBow's Review, XXXVI (September, 1867), 250.

[16] *The Independent*, April 4, 18, 1867.

Negro question lies at the bottom of our reverses . . . thousands have turned against us because we purpose to enfranchise the Blacks. . . . We have lost votes in the Free States by daring to be just to the Negro."[17] The *Independent* was quite as frank. "Negro suffrage, as a political issue," it admitted, "never before was put so squarely to certain portions of the Northern people as during the late campaigns. The result shows that the Negro is still an unpopular man."[18] Jay Cooke, the conservative financier, wrote John Sherman that he "felt a sort of intuition of coming disaster — probably growing out of a consciousness that other people would feel just as I did — disgust and mortification at the vagaries into which extremists in the Republican ranks were leading the party."[19]

To the South the northern elections seemed a confirmation of their hopes and suspicions. They overlooked the impact of the sharp commercial and industrial recession of 1867 that probably accounted for much of the Republican reverses in the fall elections. The old voices of defiance and resistance, silent or subdued since March, were lifted again. They had been right all along, they said. Congress did not speak the true sentiment of the North on the Negro and Reconstruction. President Johnson had been the true prophet. The correct strategy was not to seek the Negro vote but to suppress it, not to comply with the Reconstruction acts but to subvert them. The New York *Times* thought that "The Southern people seem to have become quite beside themselves in consequence of the *quasi* Democratic victories" in the North, and that there was "neither sense nor sanity in their exultations."[20] Moderates such as Governor James W. Throckmorton of Texas, who declared he "had advocated publicly and privately a compliance

---

[17] Quoted in *ibid.*, November 21, 1867.

[18] *Ibid.*, November 14, 1867.

[19] Jay Cooke to John Sherman, October 12, 1867, John Sherman Papers # 28298, Library of Congress.

[20] New York *Times*, October 19, 1867.

with the Sherman Reconstruction Bill," were now "determined to defeat" compliance and to leave "no stone unturned" in their efforts.[21]

The standard southern reply to northern demands was the endlessly reiterated charge of hypocrisy. Northern radicals, as a Memphis conservative put it, were "seeking to fasten what they themselves repudiate with loathing upon the unfortunate people of the South." And he pointed to the succession of northern states that had voted on and defeated Negro suffrage.[22] A Raleigh editor ridiculed Republicans of the Pennsylvania legislature who voted 29 to 13 against the franchise for Negroes. "This is a direct confession, by Northern Radicals," he added, "that they refuse to grant in Pennsylvania the '*justice*' they would enforce on the South. . . . And this is Radical meanness and hypocrisy — this their love for the negro."[23]

There was little in the Republican presidential campaign of 1868 to confute the southern charge of hypocrisy. The Chicago platform of May on which General Grant was nominated contained as its second section this formulation of the double standard of racial morality: "The guaranty by Congress of equal suffrage to all loyal men at the South was demanded by every consideration of public safety, of gratitude, and of justice, and must be maintained; while the question of suffrage in all the loyal [i.e., northern] States properly belongs to the people of those States." Thus Negro *dis*franchisement was assured in the North along with enfranchisement in the South. No direct mention of the Negro was made in the platform, nor was there mention of schools or homesteads for freedmen. Neither Grant nor his running mate Schuyler Colfax was known for any personal commitment to Negro rights, and Re-

---

[21] James W. Throckmorton to B. H. Epperson, December 19, 1867, B. H. Epperson Papers, University of Texas Archives.

[22] Memphis *Avalanche*, November 10, 1867.

[23] Raleigh *Daily Sentinel*, March 11, 1868.

publican campaign speeches in the North generally avoided the issue of Negro suffrage.

Congress acted to readmit seven of the reconstructed states to the Union in time for them to vote in the presidential election and contribute to the Republic majority. In attaching conditions to readmission, however, Congress deliberately refrained from specifying state laws protecting Negroes against discrimination in jury duty, officeholding, education, intermarriage, and a wide range of political and civil rights. By a vote of 30 to 5 the Senate defeated a bill attaching to the admission of Arkansas the condition that "no person on account of race or color shall be excluded from the benefits of education, or be deprived of an equal share of the moneys or other funds created or used by public authority to promote education. . . ."[24]

Not until the election of 1868 was safely behind them did the Republicans come forward with proposals of national action on Negro suffrage that was to result in the Fifteenth Amendment. They were extremely sensitive to northern opposition to enfranchisement. By 1869 only seven northern states had voluntarily acted to permit the Negro to vote, and no state with a substantial Negro population outside the South had done so. Except for Minnesota and Iowa, which had only a handful of Negroes, Nebraska, which entered the Union with Negro suffrage as a congressional requirement, and Wisconsin by decision of her Supreme Court, every postwar effort to enfranchise the Negro in northern states had gone down to defeat.

As a consequence moderates and conservatives among Republicans took over and dominated the framing of the Fifteenth Amendment and very strongly left their imprint on the

---

[24] *The Political History of the United States . . . During . . . Reconstruction*, ed. Edward McPherson (Washington, D.C., 1871), pp. 337–41.

measure. Even the incorrigibly radical Wendell Phillips
yielded to their sway. Addressing other radicals he pled, ". . .
for the first time in our lives we beseech them to be a little
more politicians and a little less reformers." The issue lay between the moderates and the radicals. The former wanted a
limited, negative amendment that would not confer suffrage on the freedmen, would not guarantee the franchise
and take positive steps to protect it, but would merely pro-
hibit its denial on the grounds of race and previous condition. The radicals demanded positive and firm guarantees,
federal protection, and national control of suffrage. They
would take away state control, North as well as South. They
fully anticipated and warned of all the elaborate devices that
states might resort to — and eventually did resort to —in order
to disfranchise the Negro without violating the proposed
amendment. These included such methods — later made famous — as the literacy and property tests, the understanding
clause, the poll tax, as well as elaborate and difficult registra-
tion tricks and handicaps. But safeguards against them were
all rejected by the moderates. Only four votes could be mustered for a bill to guarantee equal suffrage to all states, North
as well as South. "This [Fifteenth] amendment," said its moderate proponent Oliver P. Morton, "leaves the whole power in
the State as it exists, now, except that colored men shall not be
disfranchised for the three reasons of race, color, or previous
condition of slavery." And he added significantly, "They may,
perhaps, require property or educational tests." [25] Such tests
were already in existence in Massachusetts and other northern
states, and the debate made it perfectly apparent what might
be expected to happen later in the South.

It was little wonder that southern Republicans, already
faced with aggression against Negro voters and terribly ap-

---

[25] Quoted in Henry, "Radical Republican Policy Toward the Negro,"
p. 255.

prehensive about the future, were intensely disappointed and unhappy about the shape the debate was taking. One of their keenest disappointments was the rejection of a clause prohibiting denial or abridgment of the right of officeholding on the ground of race. It is also not surprising that southern white conservatives, in view of these developments, were on the whole fairly relaxed about the proposed Fifteenth Amendment. The shrewder of them in fact began to wonder if the whole thing were concerned mainly, not with the Reconstruction of the South, but with maneuvers of internal politics in the northern states. After all, the Negroes were already fully enfranchised and voting regularly and solidly in all the southern states.

Were there other motives behind the Fifteenth Amendment? The evidence is somewhat inferential, but a recent study has drawn attention to the significance of the closely divided vote in such states as Indiana, Ohio, Connecticut, New York, and Pennsylvania. The Negro population of these states was small, of course, but so closely was the white electorate in them divided between the two major parties that a small Negro vote could often make the difference between victory and defeat. It was assumed, of course, that this potential Negro vote would be reliably Republican. Enfranchisement by state action had been defeated in those states, and federal action seemed the only way. There is no doubt that there was idealistic support for Negro enfranchisement, especially among antislavery people in the North. But it was not the antislavery idealists who shaped the Fifteenth Amendment and guided it through Congress. The effective leaders of legislative action were moderates with practical political considerations in mind — particularly that thin margin of difference in partisan voting strength in certain northern states. They had their way, and they relentlessly voted down all measures of the sort the idealists such as Senator

Sumner were demanding.[26] For successful adoption the
amendment required ratification by twenty-eight states.
Ratification would therefore have been impossible without
support from the southern states, and an essential part of that
had to come by requiring ratification as a condition of readmission of Virginia, and perhaps of Mississippi and Georgia
as well.[27]

The Fifteenth Amendment has often been read as evidence
of renewed notice to the South of the North's firmness of purpose, as proof of its determination not to be cheated of its
idealistic war aims, as a solemn rededication to those aims.
Read more carefully, however, the Fifteenth Amendment reveals more deviousness than clarity of purpose, more partisan needs than idealistic aims, more timidity than boldness.

Signals of faltering purpose in the North such as the Fifteenth Amendment and state elections in 1867 were not lost
on the South. They were carefully weighed for their implications for the strategy of resistance. The movement of counter
Reconstruction was already well under way by the time the
amendment was ratified in March, 1870, and in that year it
took on new life in several quarters. Fundamentally it was a
terroristic campaign of underground organizations, the Ku
Klux Klan and several similar ones, for the intimidation of Republican voters and officials, the overthrow of their power,
and the destruction of their organization. Terrorists used violence of all kinds, including murder by mob, by drowning, by
torch; they whipped, they tortured, they maimed, they muti-
lated. It became perfectly clear that federal intervention of a
determined sort was the only means of suppressing the movement and protecting the freedmen in their civil and political
rights.

---

[26] William Gillette, *The Right to Vote: Politics and the Passage of the
Fifteenth Amendment* (Baltimore, 1965), *passim*.

[27] *Ibid.*, p. 100.

To meet this situation Congress passed the Enforcement Act of May 30, 1870, and followed it with the Second Enforcement Act and the Ku Klux Klan Act of 1871. These acts on the face of it would seem to have provided full and adequate machinery for the enforcement of the Fifteenth Amendment and the protection of the Negro and white Republican voters. They authorized the President to call out the Army and Navy and suspend the writ of habeas corpus; they empowered federal troops to implement court orders; and they reserved to the federal courts exclusive jurisdiction in all suffrage cases. The enforcement acts have gone down in history with the stereotypes "infamous" and "tyranical" tagged to them. As a matter of fact they were consistent with tradition and with democratic principle. Surviving remnants of them were invoked to authorize federal intervention at Little Rock in 1957 and at Oxford, Mississippi, in 1962. They are echoed in the Civil Rights Acts of 1957 and 1960, and they are surpassed in the powers conferred by the Civil Rights Act of 1964 and the Voting Rights Act of 1965.

Surely this impressive display of federal power and determination backed by gleaming steel and judicial majesty might be assumed to have been enough to bring the South to its senses and dispel forever the fantasies of southern intransigents. And in fact historians have in the main endorsed the assumption that the power of the Klan was broken by the impact of the so-called Force bills.

The truth is that while the Klan was nominally dissolved the campaign of violence, terror, and intimidation went forward save temporarily in places where federal power was displayed and so long as it was sustained. For all the efforts of the Department of Justice the deterioration of the freedman's status and the curtailment and denial of his suffrage continued steadily and rapidly. Federal enforcement officials met with impediments of all sorts. A close study of their efforts reveals that "In virtually every Southern state . . . federal deputy marshals, supervisors of elections, or soldiers were arrested by local law enforcement officers on charges ranging from false arrest or assault and battery to murder." [28]

The obvious course for the avoidance of local passions was to remove cases to federal courts for trial, as provided under a section of the First Enforcement Act. But in practice this turned out to be "exceedingly difficult." And the effort to find juries that would convict proved often to be all but impossible, however carefully they were chosen, and with whatever admixture of color. The most overwhelming evidence of guilt proved unavailing at times. Key witnesses under intimidation simply refused to testify, and those that did were known to meet with terrible reprisals. The law authorized the organization of the *posse comitatus* and the use of troops to protect juries and witnesses. But in practice the local recruits were reluctant or unreliable, and federal troops were few and remote and slow to come, and the request for them was wrapped in endless red tape and bureaucratic frustration. [29]

All these impediments to justice might have been overcome had sufficient money been made available by Congress. And right at this crucial point once again the northern will and purpose flagged and failed the cause they professed to sustain. It is quite clear where the blame lies. Under the new laws the cost of maintaining courts in the most affected districts of the South soared tremendously, quadrupled in some. Yet Congress starved the courts from the start, providing only about 1,000,000 dollars a year — far less than was required. The Attorney General had to cut corners, urge economy, and in

---

[28] Everette Swinney, "Enforcing the Fifteenth Amendment, 1870–1877," *Journal of Southern History*, XXVIII (May, 1962), 210.
[29] *Ibid.*, pp. 210–11.

1873 instruct district attorneys to prosecute no case "unless the public interest imperatively demands it." An antiquated judicial structure proved wholly inadequate to handle the extra burden and clear their dockets. "If it takes a court over one month to try five offenders," asked the Attorney General concerning 420 indictments in South Carolina, "how long will it take to try four hundred, already indicted, and many hundreds more who deserve to be indicted?" He thought it "obvious that the attempt to bring to justice even a small portion of the guilty in that state must fail" under the circumstances. Quite apart from the inadequacy and inefficiency of the judicial structure, it is of significance that a majority of the Department of Justice officers in the South at this time, despite the carpetbagger infusion, were southern-born. A study by Everette Swinney concludes that "Some marshals and district attorneys were either sensitive to Southern public opinion or in substantial agreement with it." The same has been found true of numbers of federal troops and their officers on duty in the South.[30] Then in 1874 an emasculating opinion from the Supreme Court by Justice Joseph P. Bradley in *United States* v. *Cruikshank et al.* cast so much doubt on the constitutionality of the Enforcement Acts as to render successful prosecutions virtually impossible.

There is also sufficient evidence in existence to raise a question about how much the Enforcement Acts were intended for application in the policing of elections in the South all along, as against their possible application in other quarters of the Union. As it turned out, nearly half of the cost of policing was applied to elections of New York City, where Democratic bosses gave the opposition much trouble. Actually the bulk of federal expenditures under the Enforcement Acts was made in the North, which leads one student to conclude that their primary object from the start was not the distraught South un-

---

[30] *Ibid.*, pp. 212–16.

der Reconstruction, but the urban strongholds of the Democrats in the North.[31] Once again, as with the purposes behind the Fifteenth Amendment, one is left to wonder how much radical Reconstruction was really concerned with the South and how much with the party needs of the Republicans in the North.

Finally, to take a longer view, it is only fair to allow that if ambiguous and partisan motives in the writing and enforcement of Reconstruction laws proved to be the seeds of failure in American race policy for earlier generations, those same laws and constitutional amendments eventually acquired a wholly different significance for the race policy of a later generation. The laws outlasted the ambiguities of their origins. It is, in fact, impossible to account for such limited successes as the Second Reconstruction can claim without acknowledging its profound indebtedness to the First.

---

[31] Robert A. Horn, "National Control of Congressional Elections" (unpublished Ph.D. dissertation, Princeton, N.J., 1942).

Comment on
C. Vann Woodward's Paper

RUSSEL B. NYE
Michigan State University

It seems fitting that the final paper of the conference should treat of this quite specific problem that the politicians of the Reconstruction period faced — what to do about translating the rhetoric of debate and the suffering of war into actual, practical, political fact. Because this most certainly was the problem — now that it was all over, and the slave freed, what to do about it? Professor Woodward's exposition of the impact of racial theories on radical political policy and their effect on the necessities of party politics makes its point well. It would be tempting to draw parallels, for the popular notion that history repeats itself is an attractive one; however, I should rather comment on some of the general implications inherent in this particular political aspect of the racial issue as it appeared in the Reconstruction period, placing Professor Woodward's paper within the context of the kind of American reform operative at the time.

American reform during the early years of the nineteenth century — or, to be more precise, during its great burgeoning in the third, fourth, and fifth decades — was a pervasive movement that swept everything into it, from crusades for good digestion, Sabbath reform, and a twelve-hour day to a state of spiritual communion with God. James Russell Lowell remarked of this reforming zeal, "Every possible form of intellectual and physical dyspepsia brought forth its gospel. No brain but had its private maggot." But all these reforms, crackpot as some of them seemed to be, Lowell recognized as "part of a great struggle for fresh air," a struggle to express in society something of what Emerson called "the infinite worthiness of man." The cause of the slave, at first only a small and least fashionable one of this great stirring of humanitarianism, gradually absorbed and eclipsed all the rest. Its appeal was wide, its leadership shrewd, its relation to politics direct, its relevance to the future of democracy unmistakable. The whole cause of American reform became closely bound up with the place and the rights of the Negro in American society; the political and constitutional problem of whether the nation could continue to exist half slave and half free was itself based on a deeper issue of Negro and human rights. No reform in American history encompassed so many people or generated so much power for change. Yet the guns were hardly cool before these once-flaming issues of Negro and human rights virtually disappeared, pushed hurriedly to one side not only by politicians but by reformers, apparently, themselves. The story of postwar reform, as it affected the Negro, is one of inconsistency, maneuver, confusion, even betrayal.

The question is, of course, why? The great antislavery crusade once produced great heat and power; where did it go? Whereas the antislavery movement once had no dearth of leaders, there seemed to be few, or none, to continue after emancipation had been won. Whereas the issue of Negro rights had been a primary force in prewar reform on a dozen fronts, it showed no such power after the war.

One reason is clear. The antislavery movement was more concerned with slavery than with the slave, involved with the abstraction of the institution rather than with the individuality of its components. Far from tempering or changing traditionally held American attitudes toward the Negro, neither the prewar controversy over slavery nor the military conflict which it helped to produce changed those attitudes to any degree.

The racist theory developed by the prewar supporters of slavery was never seriously challenged by the abolitionists or by the reconstructionists, neither of whom framed any satisfactory answers to the accepted versions of racial differences developed by Nott, Cartwright, Van Evrie, and the other racially oriented writers of the early nineteenth century. The anthropology with which the nineteenth century had to work simply did not provide any real reason for granting the Negro those rights that freedom presumably bestowed upon him. Practically every literate northerner and southerner believed more or less what the proslavery scientist, Dr. Joseph Clark Nott of Alabama, taught in his *Two Lectures on the Natural History of the Caucasian and Negro Races* (Mobile, Ala., 1844), that the Negro was an inferior race, incapable of ever attaining equality with the white. The work of European racists such as Count Arthur Gobineau, whose *Essay on the Inequality of Races* Nott himself helped to translate in its 1860 edition, and Houston Chamberlin in his *Foundations of the Nineteenth Century* (New York, 1911) served to substantiate what earlier racist theories maintained. William Chambers, an English traveler who toured the United States in 1855, remarked that in every section of the country, North and South, it was "a fixed notion . . . that the coloured is by nature a subordinate race." Had Chambers repeated his tour in 1875 or 1895, he would have found no reason to change his opinion.

During the Reconstruction years these carefully established

and widely held concepts of race encountered little opposition. In fact, there was even a resurgence of racism toward the close of the century, buttressed by the work of such people as Madison Grant, Lothrop Stoddard, and the violently racist novelist Thomas Dixon. Nott's book, *The Types of Mankind* (Philadelphia), written in 1854 with G. R. Glidden, was still selling well in its ninth edition in 1900, while Grant's *Passing of the Great Race* (New York, 1916) and Stoddard's *Rising Tide of Color* (New York, 1920) reinforced all the old theories. Not many listened to the anthropologists and archeologists who were demolishing the racist myth — William G. Ripley, Franz Boas, J. H. Breasted, and others. South Carolina's Senator McLaurin and Massachusetts' Senator Hoar no doubt reflected the majority opinion when they agreed unctuously during the nineties on "the divine right of the Caucasian to govern the inferior races" at home and abroad.

Obviously, there could be no real shift in the political or social position of the Negro in American life until there had been a change in those racial theories which traditionally determined that position. Such a change was not forthcoming in 1865, or for a long time. What lies beneath the politics of the Reconstruction period, so far as it touched the Negro, is the prevailing racist policy tacitly accepted by both parties and by the general public. Whatever commitment the federal government gave to Negro rights by the Fourteenth Amendment, the Enforcement Acts of 1870 and 1871, the Civil Rights Act of 1875, and so on, the commitment was not based on any widely accepted belief that the Negro was equal. A great deal is known about the connections of racism and imperialism during these decades; we need to know much more about the connection between racism and practical politics. The politics of Reconstruction existed within a framework of racial theories which had not changed since the early nineteenth century (or the eighteenth, for that matter), which is a fact of importance in interpreting it.

On the other hand, the politics of the Reconstruction period also existed within a framework of reform which had changed, quite sharply, since the days of Weld, Garrison, Phillips, and the abolitionists. This too is a fact of importance. One can *feel* the difference in the reform movements of the late nineteenth century; it is not always easy to locate and define, but it is there. There are few echoes of the blazing rhetoric of reform during the seventies. Instead of the incendiary journalism of Garrison or Goodell, one finds, after the war, the reasoned judgment of E. L. Godkin, surely no retrograde Bourbon, who concluded in *The Nation* (XXXI [1880], 126) that he could not visualize placing trust in "the hands of a class without property, without education, and without a single political habit or tradition."

I quote Godkin because I think that the key to an understanding of the changed ambiance of the kind of reforms that surrounded the whole racial question in the Reconstruction period lies in that word *government*. The issue of Negro rights and his position in society before 1860 was placed within a *moral* context; the same issue after 1865 existed within a *political* context. The Negro was no longer a problem in morality, but a problem in politics. This is important, for I think it accounts for the fact that it is virtually impossible to find any leader in public life, political or otherwise, who after 1866 committed himself with real *moral* fervor to the Negro's cause. Leadership changed in postwar society from crusaders to caucuses, from reformers to realists; the appeal was no longer to conscience but to consensus.

This happened because the problem of Negro rights during the latter portion of the nineteenth century was related to a quite different concept of reform than it was a half-century earlier. Because American reform itself changed in quality between 1860 and 1880, the issue of the Negro could elicit one kind of response from reformers before the Civil War, and quite another kind from the generation after it.

The reform movement with which the cause of the slave merged in the forties was intensely religious, personal, and antipolitical. To the crusader of Garrison's time, changes in society came about by reason of changes wrought in the individual. Social wrongs were righted by personal rectification; improved men made a better society; good men made good institutions. This kind of reform, swept along with the prevailing currents of romanticism and evangelism, conceived its solutions to social problems in internal terms. Slavery was to be abolished by appealing to the consciences of slaveholders; Negro rights might be secured by appealing to Christians' sense of brotherhood in God. These reformers did not trust organizations and they did not trust politics — indeed, many virtually rejected it. Thoreau advocated civil disobedience and Garrison disunion; Lowell seceded from the Mexican War and Emerson refused to recognize the legality of the Fugitive Slave Act. The way to reform lay not through the apparatus of politics; it lay in detonating what Lowell called "that kernel of deadly explosiveness" within the individual. Not only was this kind of reform personal, it was also comprehensive. Reformers like Gerrit Smith or Parker Pillsbury or William Goodell might be involved in a half-dozen reforms at once. All reforms were conceived of as parts of one great overriding reform, which was simply to make society perfect.

Later nineteenth-century reform was not this way. It was less individualistic, less subjective, much more institutionally and politically oriented, much more selective and aimed at narrower targets — such as civil service, taxes, money, monopoly, railroads, wages, and working hours. Reform was not so personalized, not so motivated as before by inward emotional drives; it was likely to be concerned with machinery as much as with morality. To the reformer of the seventies and after, legislation seemed the most powerful tool in his arsenal and government the chief vehicle by which his reform could be effectuated. He might want to "change the minds and consciences of men" as Channing had, but he was more concerned with passing statutes like the Pendleton Act or the Granger laws to take care of those whose consciences did not properly respond. The symbolic reformer of this period was not a Garrison or a Noyes or a Dorothea Dix, but Ward or Ely or Ross. The great reform document of the times could not be something like *Uncle Tom's Cabin*, but was more likely to be something like Lincoln Steffens' *Shame of the Cities*.

This kind of reform operated at a much lower temperature than the reform of the early nineteenth century and required a different kind of leader. The spokesman of the gentleman reformers of these decades was E. L. Godkin; their political hero, Grover Cleveland; their intellectual, Henry Adams; their organizers, such men as Charles Eliot Norton, George William Curtis, Charles Francis Adams, Jr. The difference is that, I suppose, of the thermal content of the American Anti-Slavery Society under Garrison and the Social Science Association under Charles Francis Adams. The point is that within this kind of reform, directed at the targets it selected and with this kind of reformer leading it, the cause of the freed Negro had little place.

There were a variety of reasons for the changes in the reform tradition that took place after 1860, too many for a full discussion here. Some of these changes had already begun by the time of the Civil War, and no doubt would have continued as effectively without it. There were two major factors, however, in postwar American society which had perhaps more to do than any others with the transformation of the native reform tradition.

First, in the United States the alliance of business and government was never so powerful as in this period; nowhere were the rights of capital and property so firmly established as benchmarks of measurement in law, politics, education, religion, and social thought. Curiously enough, this consolidation of government and business for a long time created no strong or unified radical reform in opposition to it. Instead, reform protests came from a number of interest groups, each concerned with a particular issue growing out of its special interest. The reformers — and there were many dedicated ones — met at no common point, though their interests might run parallel. Reform during the Reconstruction years was not an over-all movement, but a fragmentation of groups. Reform in politics, for example, divided itself among liberal Republicans, Populists, Prohibitionists, National Labor Reform, Anti-Monopoly, Greenbackers, Independent Labor groups and the Union Labor party, the Equal Rights group, and lesser factions. No single reform — as abolition once had — appeared to touch and attract them all. There was nothing to combine the forces represented by such diverse figures as Godkin, Donnelly, Schurz, Altgeld, Lloyd, Adams, Foulke, Russell, and Mary Ellen Lease, to name a few. The united front was on the other side of the street.

Second, Social Darwinism confronted American reform with a solid ideological wall. Spencer was more popular in America than anywhere else. His disciples, among them such influential men as William Graham Sumner, Andrew Carnegie, and E. L. Youmans, spread Spencerian ethics everywhere. When Spencer wrote that "the truth is that the social order is fixed by laws of nature precisely analogous to those of the physical order," and concluded that "the most that man can do . . . by his ignorance and conceit is to mar the operation of social laws," he virtually closed the door on the possibility of reform as the earlier nineteenth century conceived it. Had all reformers accepted Spencer, reform would have stopped, for there was obviously nothing to be gained by interfering with the laws of Nature. Many did not, but, at the least, Spencer's version of applied Darwinism reduced the impetus and changed the direction of American reform for a generation and more to come. What Social Darwinism had to say, of course, also had implications for the position of the Negro in society, for if the Negro were inferior, he clearly could not compete equally in the Darwinian race, nor should he. The idea of equality — among races or men — Sumner found "inherently absurd." Lothrop Stoddard, who tied his own violent racist theory neatly into the same bundle with Spencerian ethics, thought the idea of equality "one of the most pernicious delusions that ever afflicted mankind." The nature and extent of the impact of popular acceptance of Social Darwinism on political thought and action in the Reconstruction period needs, it seems to me, a good deal of further exploration.

To conclude, Professor Woodward's paper opens a number of interesting avenues. We need not be surprised at the fact that the Negro did not obtain the rights or the status during Reconstruction which the abolitionists once claimed he should have. His rights and his status were never so primary a part of controversy as they seemed to be, and the ease with which they were abandoned after 1865 is ample proof of it. Neither the antislavery controversy, nor the Civil War, nor the inconclusive political maneuvering of Reconstruction, made any basic changes in the prevailing attitudes toward race, North and South — attitudes clearly reflected in the congressional politics of Reconstruction. The study of the politics of the period, particularly as it touches on the status and rights of the Negro, must be made within the context of the changed nature and direction of the reform tradition as it developed in the latter decades of the century.